I0090504

FUTURE-PROOFING

YOUR

SDA

BUSINESS

COMPILED BY TANIA GOMEZ

🐢 TurtlePublishing

Copyright © 2025 Tania Gomez

All rights reserved. No part of this publication may be reproduced, stored in a retrieval system, or transmitted in any form or by any means, electronic, mechanical, photocopying, recording or otherwise, without prior written permission of the author.

Legal Notice: This book is copyright protected. This book is only for personal use. You cannot amend, distribute, sell, use, quote or paraphrase any part, or the content within this book, without the consent of the author or publisher.

Disclaimer: Please note the information contained within this document is for educational and entertainment purposes only. All effort has been executed to present accurate, up to date, and reliable, complete information. No warranties of any kind are declared or implied. Readers acknowledge that the authors are not engaging in the rendering of legal, financial, medical or professional advice. The content within this book has been derived from various sources. Please consult a licensed professional before attempting any techniques outlined in this book.

By reading this document, the reader agrees that under no circumstances is the author responsible for any losses, direct or indirect, which are incurred as a result of the use of the information contained within this document, including, but not limited to — errors, omissions, or inaccuracies.

Published by Turtle Publishing
Cover & Interior Design by Kathy Shanks

ISBN: 978-1-7643960-7-3 (paperback)
ISBN: 978-1-7643960-8-0 (ebook)

TurtlePublishing
turtlepublishing.com.au

To my SDA provider clients and to the ecosystem that works so hard to create real impact for people with disability. A house and a home are not the same thing. Anyone can build a structure. It takes vision, integrity, and heart to build a home. This book is for those of you who carry that responsibility with pride. For the providers, builders, designers, investors, assessors, and advocates who refuse to cut corners and who understand that what you build changes lives.

TABLE OF CONTENTS

PART 2
FROM PLANS TO PRACTICE

PART 3
THE ROAD AHEAD—DEMAND, DATA, AND SYSTEM CHANGE

INTRODUCTION

By *Tania Gomez*

I've worked in the NDIS space for a long time. Before that, I was a special needs teacher. Sat on the board of disability providers under the block funded model, Then a consultant. Then an auditor. I've seen this sector from all angles: on the floor, in the boardroom, and in the middle of tough audits where everything's on the line.

I thought I understood the NDIS. Then I entered the world of SDA.

Even with all my experience, I found SDA confusing. The amount of regulation, the number of stakeholders, the constant changes. It was hard to figure out who did what, what good looked like, or even where to start. It felt like a completely different language.

So I did what I always do when I feel out of my depth—I asked questions. I launched the SDA Mastery podcast and started talking to people who were already in it: the developers, providers, designers, investors, clinicians, and participants who were living it every day. I wanted to know what worked, what didn't, and what they wished someone had told them earlier.

This book came from those conversations. Many of the people I interviewed have become its co-authors. It's a collaboration. A shared effort. A field guide built from experience, not theory.

It was written at a time when SDA was in the news for all the wrong reasons. We've seen blanket accusations, political finger-pointing, and good providers being lumped in with the bad ones. It's disheartening, especially when you know how many people are genuinely trying to do the right thing, even when the system makes that hard.

This book is for those people—the ones who want to deliver SDA that works. The ones who have invested their time, money, and energy into making housing something better. The ones who are learning as they go and just want something real to lean on.

Below is a quick look at who you'll hear from in this book, what each chapter covers, and one quote that really stuck with me.

What You'll Find in This Book

We've broken the book into three parts, based on the natural stages of SDA delivery: from vision and design to day-to-day practice, to the bigger picture of where we're heading. Each section explores a different layer of the SDA journey, with voices from across the sector who've lived it, built it, and are still learning through it.

Part 1: Beyond the Build

This section explores what good SDA looks like beyond just ticking compliance boxes. It dives into the intent behind SDA, what design should actually achieve, and the structural barriers that keep us from getting there. These chapters are about shifting our thinking from rules to outcomes, and from houses to homes.

- **Chapter 1–Joseph Connellan: What Good Disability Housing Looks Like**

  'There is no point in having a compliant house that doesn't actually meet the needs of the person it was designed for.'

  Joseph lays the foundation for understanding what good SDA should look like. He breaks down the gap between regulation and reality and shows how to move from minimum standards to meaningful outcomes.

- **Chapter 2–Dr Dinesh Palipana: Creating More Than Housing**

  'When homes are designed with people in mind, they give you freedom. When they're not, they trap you in the very place you're supposed to feel safest.'

  Dinesh shares his lived experience and clinical insight to highlight why SDA must go beyond physical structure and become a tool for independence, dignity, and hope.

- **Chapter 3–Keira Nicholson: Designing SDA That Gets Built**

  'Planning is where good design goes to die. Without reform, we'll keep building the wrong thing in the wrong place.'

  Keira takes us behind the scenes of SDA development. She explains how planning systems, funding rules, and misaligned priorities can stall projects before they even begin.

Part 2: From Plans to Practice

Once the build is complete, the real work begins. This section is about what happens on the ground. How providers meet standards, manage tenancies, and create homes that hold. These chapters give a raw and practical view of delivering SDA in real life.

- **Chapter 4—Bruce Bromley: Designing for Dignity**

  'Good design is invisible. You only notice it when it's missing.'

  Bruce draws from years of on-the-ground experience to explore what dignity looks like in practice. This chapter shows how empathy in design leads to spaces that feel like home.

- **Chapter 5—Tania Gomez: Navigating SDA Standards**

  'The standards aren't there to trip you up. They're there to help you build something solid if you know how to use them.'

  I break down the five SDA Practice Standards in plain English. This chapter is about turning compliance from a stress point into a strength and making the rules work for you.

- **Chapter 6—Perry Klepe: The Realities of Being an SDA Provider**

  'You don't know what you don't know until you're in it. Then you realise how much is at stake.'

  Perry shares the emotional and practical reality of stepping into SDA as a new provider. It's honest, raw, and full of insight for anyone thinking of doing the same.

Part 3: The Road Ahead: Demand, Data, and System Change

This final section zooms out. It looks at the broader SDA ecosystem: how we collect and use data, fund development, connect with supports, and scale quality without losing sight of the participant. These chapters push us to think long-term and system-wide.

- **Chapter 7–Hong Knowling: SDA Demand and Data Using Data to Deliver Smarter SDA Housing**

  'The data looks fine on a spreadsheet, but it doesn't reflect what people are actually asking for.'

  Hong challenges the assumptions behind supply and demand forecasts. She explains where the real gaps are and how better data could help us build smarter, not just more.

- **Chapter 8–Brad Fuller: Unlocking Supply Through Smarter Investment**

  'Impact and return don't have to compete. You can design for both.'

  Brad shares how the right funding models can drive both financial and participant outcomes. He unpacks the investor mindset and shows how alignment can unlock more supply.

- **Chapter 9–Debbie Kindness: Rethinking the SDA Ecosystem**

  'You can't just hand someone a house and call it support. Housing needs to connect with everything else.'

  Debbie explains why SDA can't be treated in isolation. She advocates for integrated approaches that connect housing with the broader support ecosystem.

- **Chapter 10—Angad Singh: Developing Quality SDA Homes**

  'You don't scale quality by accident. It takes structure, discipline, and a lot of listening.'

  Angad walks through what it takes to deliver high-quality SDA projects at scale, from risk management to participant voice. This chapter is a practical guide to doing SDA well.

At Tania Gomez Consulting, everything we do comes back to three things: educate, inspire, and connect. That's because most providers aren't just looking for answers; they're looking for support, clarity, and someone to help them figure out what's next.

In 2024 and 2025, more than 10,000 NDIS providers showed up at our events. Over 145,000 podcast episodes have been downloaded. That tells me something loud and clear—providers aren't giving up. They're trying. They're learning. They want to do better, even when the system makes it hard.

This book is for them. For you. For every person out there trying to make SDA work in real life and improve the quality of disability housing.

To the incredible co-authors who gave their time, experience, and honesty to this project, thank you. Your insights, your generosity, and your willingness to speak the truth are what make this book what it is. I'm grateful to have walked this road with you.

There's an African proverb I love that says, 'If you want to go fast, go alone. If you want to go far, go together.' This book is proof of what's possible when we choose to go far together, to improve disability housing and the people it's designed to support.

Tania Gomez

PART 1

BEYOND THE BUILD

Designing with dignity,
intention, and purpose.

*'Design is not just what it looks like
and feels like. Design is how it works.'*
—Steve Jobs

CHAPTER 1

WHAT GOOD HOUSING FOR PEOPLE WITH DISABILITY LOOKS LIKE

BY JOSEPH CONNELLAN

Joseph Connellan is an experienced non-profit director with a career spanning more than 35 years across the Victorian housing, homelessness, and disability sectors. He's held leadership roles in government, mutuals, and not-for-profit organisations, with a longstanding focus on the intersection between housing and services for people with disability.

Now retired from consultancy, Joseph continues to contribute through writing and creative projects. He's authored numerous analytical works on disability and housing policy and practice, bringing clarity to complex systems and advocating for meaningful change.

In 2022, he published his debut novel.

• • •

CONNECT WITH JOSEPH AT:
WEBSITE: josephconnellan.com
LINKED IN: @joseph-connellan-78ba3b18

The Illusion of Good Housing

When people say 'disability housing', they're usually talking about something that meets the Specialised Disability Accommodation (SDA) standards. A compliant build, signed off by an assessor, sitting in the right design category.

However, I prefer to use the term 'housing for people with disability'. The housing itself isn't disabled. The person is central, not the building. That change in language helps shift the whole conversation because once you start with people, you look at housing differently.

Good housing isn't about compliance; it's about whether someone can live in it safely, stay there over time, and get the support they need. A house might be compliant and still completely useless. That's the core problem. We've created a system that rewards development outcomes, not housing outcomes.

I've been in this space for a long time—over 35 years—working across housing, disability services, and government. I've run community housing providers, managed the housing of people who have moved out of institutions, worked inside government policy teams, and advised on NDIS housing frameworks. I've seen how the big programs are designed, and I've seen what happens when they hit the ground.

The SDA program was meant to improve access to housing for people with significant disability. It was projected to house around 28,000 people and replace the non-contemporary housing of the 17,500 who were living in SDA-like accommodation. Today, it only houses about 15,000. Around 9000 people have SDA funding sitting in their plan, but they're not using it. In real terms, SDA houses fewer people now than when the program started.

SDA has been misclassified from the start. It's been treated like a housing product in an open market when it should have been funded like infrastructure. It's scarce, complex, geographically constrained, and tied to high-value support. That's not a normal market; that's a program planning problem. But instead of planning, we've just been subsidising supply and hoping for the best.

The result? Oversupply and undersupply at the same time. Homes built in the wrong places. Whole streets of SDA with no one living in them. Vacant houses while people with funding sit in aged care or hospitals. Investor losses. And participants who've been promised choice, with nowhere to go.

This is one of the biggest non-government housing programs in Australian history. It should be a national success story. Instead, it's invisible and failing quietly in the background while the rest of the NDIS gets the headlines.

I'm not writing this chapter to critique the system; I'm writing it because we can do better. And we already know how.

In the pages ahead, I'll set out a way to think about good housing. I'll explain the five barriers that stop people from getting and keeping a home. I'll outline the difference between what's technically compliant and what actually works. I'll point to where things have gone wrong. And I'll propose a clear, simple four-step fix to get SDA working again.

But before we go there, we need to talk about who this housing is for. Because unless we define that, we're not designing for anyone.

Who This Housing is Really For

There are 5.5 million people in Australia who identify as having a disability. That includes everything from chronic illness to mobility restrictions to sensory or cognitive impairment. It's a very broad category.

Of those 5.5 million, about 3.2 million are under 65 years old. Within that group, around 1.1 million have what's called a profound or severe disability. These are people who need help with core activities like communication, mobility, or personal care. That's where the NDIS focuses.

The NDIS currently supports about 750,000 people. So, we've already gone from 5.5 million to 750,000. But when we talk about housing, the group is smaller again.

There are about 41,000 people in the NDIS who need access to 24-hour support. That's the cohort that might need specialised housing, something like SDA. These are people who require support on-site or close by every day to live well in our community.

And, of the 25,000 with SDA funding, only about 15,000 of them are housed in SDA.

Here's the funnel:

- 5.5 million Australians with a disability
- 3.2 million under 65
- 1.1 million with severe or profound disability
- 750,000 NDIS participants
- 41,000 who may need access to 24-hour support
- 36,000 with Supported Independent Living (SIL)
- 25,000 with SDA funding
- 15,000 housed in SDA

So when we talk about housing for people with disability it important that we identify which people with disability we are focusing on. For me it is mostly those 41,000 who may require 24 hour access to support as they are the group most likely to benefit from enhanced housing.

If you don't define the cohort properly, you can't plan. And if you can't plan, the result is what we've already got: empty homes, misused funding, and participants who still can't find a place to live.

What do We Mean by Good Housing?

Once you define who the housing is for, the next question is: what does *good* housing look like?

The answer isn't in the SDA rules. It's not in the design categories. It's not in a certification report.

Good housing overcomes any and all of the.

Five key barriers that people with disability face when it comes to housing. If a provider or developer isn't addressing the barrier or barriers that the person who lives in that house, they're not delivering good housing. It might be new. It might be architecturally interesting. It might even be certified SDA. But it won't work.

The five barriers are:

1. **Design:** This is the most obvious one. Is the property accessible? Does it match the person's functional needs? Discussions about housing for people with disability gets fixated on this, but it's only one piece of the puzzle.

2. **Location:** Even if the design is fine, it might be in the wrong place. I've seen beautiful SDA homes built in

areas with no support workers, no public transport, and no community infrastructure. That's not good housing.

3. **Affordability:** Most people with disability have modest incomes. They can't afford market rent. If the housing costs more than 30 percent of the Disability Support Pension (an affordability level used in social housing), it's probably not viable for them long-term.

4. **Support Integration:** Housing has to match the support. There's no point building a home if the support team can't deliver services there.

5. **Housing Management:** This one is ignored a lot. If a property manager doesn't understand the support model, things break down fast. You need tenancy managers who can work with support coordinators and support providers, not just collect rent.

I've seen plenty of developments that got the design right but failed on the other four. I've also seen some modest homes that weren't perfect on paper, but they worked because the support was well-integrated, the rent was manageable, and the location was spot on.

Good housing is housing that works day to day, week to week, year to year. The outcomes are simple: the person stays housed, the support works, and the system doesn't have to intervene.

If you don't address each of the individual barriers that person confronts, none of that happens.

What Good Housing Looks Like

There's no shortage of knowledge about what works. We know housing must be close to community infrastructure and support. We know tenancy needs to be actively managed, not assumed. We know new buildings don't guarantee better outcomes.

These aren't new insights. They have been there for decades.

What's different now is scale. SDA is the largest disability housing investment this country has seen. If we keep repeating the same patterns, the consequences will be harder to reverse.

The housing being built today will shape outcomes for the next 20 to 30 years. If it's in the wrong location, poorly matched to need, or unsupported, it will lock people out of the very system designed to include them.

There are SDA homes that work. They aren't always the ones in brochures. They're not always the newest or most complex. They're not always in ideal locations, but they work because the setup fits the person, the support, and the tenancy. And they hold.

I've seen housing like this. I've managed housing like this. It doesn't have to be large. It doesn't need smart-home features or expensive finishes. It needs to be stable. It needs to support the person's routine. It needs to be a place they want to stay.

What makes these homes work isn't the design specification; it's the fit. The pieces line up. The person is supported. The home is maintained. The tenancy lasts.

There are also signs you can look for. The person has stayed longer than a year. The support provider hasn't changed. The housing manager knows who to call if there's a problem. The provider and the property manager have a working relationship. When these things are in place, it holds together.

These homes aren't perfect, but they don't break. And if they do, someone notices and fixes it.

Choice matters too. Some people choose the housing from the beginning. Others move in and settle over time. Either way, there's a sense that the person belongs there. They're not just placed. They've made it work.

There's no formula for this, but there are patterns. The good ones are planned around the person. The support and the housing are designed to work together. The management is proactive. And the housing is part of a broader system that responds when things change.

This is not about innovation; it's about doing the basics properly. Not once. Not for a pilot. But consistently. And at scale.

Building for Stability and Scale

SDA was meant to be scalable. The whole program is based on the idea that housing providers, developers, and investors deliver more housing in response to demand. And we do need more housing for people with complex needs, but scaling only works if the model underneath it is stable.

Scaling means taking something that works and repeating it. It means a viable investment and management model. It means a home where the person is supported, the tenancy lasts, and the provider can continue operating without constant crisis management. That kind of housing can be delivered again in another location, or for another cohort, but if it's not working in one place, it won't work in 10.

Before you can scale, the setup has to be right. That means understanding who the housing is for. What kind of support the person needs. Whether the provider can deliver that support consistently. Whether the property manager can respond to issues. Whether the workforce is available in that location. Whether the person wants to live there.

I've seen good housing models break when providers expand into areas they don't know. The support workers aren't local. The referrals don't come through. The transport links aren't there. The homes sit vacant, even when they meet the design standard. The house is the last piece of the puzzle, not the first, and certainly not the only.

The most effective SDA providers I've seen start small. One or two homes in areas where they already have a presence. They know the services. They know the referral pathways. They know the community. They build from there.

They're also clear on their limits. If they can only manage three homes properly, they manage three. They don't build 10 and then figure it out later. They grow based on capacity, not on capital.

Partnerships can help, but only if they're real. I've seen support providers work closely with housing organisations where both sides understand their overlapping roles. They plan together. They manage risk together. They stay in contact once the tenancy starts. Those models are slow to build but easy to repeat.

Replication is what matters. A housing model that's stable and clear can be copied. You can do it again in another location. You can train staff. You can explain how it works to investors and regulators. That's scale.

But if your model depends on a handful of people holding everything together, or only works because of one well-placed coordinator, that's not a system; that's just luck. And you can't scale luck.

There's also a problem with how the current system talks about growth. A lot of developers and funders think scale means more stock. They're focused on the number of dwellings, not the outcome for the person. That's why we see so many homes in the wrong place with the wrong support, and no one able to live in them.

We don't need more of what doesn't work. We need more of what does. But you can only build that if you're honest about what your organisation can deliver. That means knowing what your team can manage. How far the property manager can travel. How many homes a support coordinator can reasonably cover. Where your workforce comes from. Who you can partner with. Whether the housing you're planning fits with local demand. You can't plan that from a desk. You have to know the place. You have to talk to the services. You have to be involved early, not once the property is built.

The SDA program has treated housing like it's something that can be scaled through design and funding, but it can't. It has to be scaled through delivery.

What Needs to Change

We know what the problem is. SDA has been set up to fund housing, not to deliver it.

We've talked about that. We've seen the results. Empty homes. People who are funded but are stuck in hospital.

Providers try to make it work without the information or partnerships they need.

The real question is: what would it look like if we got this right?

Not a new version of the same model. The current SDA funding model is framed around an open market operating with centrally set pricing. It's a highly unusual way to fund a housing program. After more than eight years of operation, we can clearly say it has failed. We need a different one. One that works and delivers the best possible housing where it's needed at the lowest sustainable price. Something simpler, more connected, and built around delivery.

Here's what needs to change.

1. Start From Real Demand, Speculation

The NDIA already knows who has SDA in their plan. It knows what they need and where they are. That data should drive development. Instead, most housing is still being built based on available land, not actual need. If providers, developers, or states want to build SDA, they should start with real demand data–shared, validated, and current. That means clarity at a Local Government level on:

- Where eligible participants are
- What support they need
- What locations they're connected to
- Who's waiting for housing now
- What housing already exists, its configuration and its condition

This is how infrastructure funding works in other sectors. We don't build schools or hospitals without understanding the population or what's already there. We shouldn't build disability housing that way either.

2. Build Partnerships That Deliver, not Just Consult

Most SDA partnerships still happen too late. Developers design and build, and then bring in support providers. That model puts all the risk at the end when the tenancy doesn't hold or the support doesn't fit.

A better model brings partners in at the start.

- The housing partner works with a provider who knows the cohort
- They plan location and layout together
- They share tenancy responsibility, not just handover

It's not about doing more consultation; it's about joint delivery. Real alignment, from the ground up.

3. Make Tenancy Part of the Model

Housing isn't just about the building or the support; it's also about tenancy. That's where everything plays out. If the tenancy is weak, the housing fails.

In working SDA models, the property is actively managed. Repairs happen quickly. The property manager understands the support needs. Issues are picked up before they escalate. Relationships matter.

This needs to be funded properly, not assumed. A functioning SDA home requires tenancy coordination. That role needs to be defined, funded, and accountable.

4. Plan for Scale Only After Stability

Scaling SDA doesn't mean building more; it means repeating what works. You can't replicate an unstable model.

Before expanding, providers need to ask:

- Does the current model hold?
- Are tenancies stable?
- Is the workforce sustainable?
- Are outcomes being tracked?

If yes, scale it slowly. If not, pause and fix it.

Scaling starts with one home that works, then another. If each one can function on its own, then it can be repeated. That's how growth should work.

5. Shift the Role of Government from Funder to Coordinator

Right now, the government is a funder and regulator. Government is also the SDA program manager, responsible for its success or failure. However, no one in Government is effectively coordinating delivery.

We don't need another agency, but we do need a clear function. That could be:

- A national team that tracks supply and demand
- A regional planner who matches housing to need
- A public dashboard that shows where housing is and what's available

Someone has to see the whole picture. Someone has to know if the model is working. If we want to stop repeating the same mistakes, we need accountability.

Conclusion

We've been talking about this for a long time. The same issues keep coming up: location, tenancy, support, fit. What's missing is a focus on delivery. Who's doing what, how it fits together, and whether it works for the person.

There's been plenty of money and plenty of interest, but outcomes haven't followed. People are still waiting. Providers are still guessing. Houses are still empty. The issue isn't the idea; the issue is how it's being delivered.

We keep talking about SDA like it's a property product, but it's not. It's a disability support solution. If the person doesn't end up living there, if the tenancy doesn't hold, then it doesn't matter how well it's designed or funded.

We need to start with a different question: can we deliver this?

That means thinking about the whole arrangement, not just the house, but the funding, the financing, the support, the tenancy, the ongoing management. It's not enough to meet the standard; it has to work for the person.

I've seen it work. I've seen housing that doesn't look impressive on paper but fits the person.

We've built some, but not enough good homes. Not because we don't know how, but because we haven't made it anyone's job.

If we want this to improve, that's where we start. With the question, 'Can we deliver this?' And with someone who stays responsible until the answer is yes.

CHAPTER 2

CREATING MORE THAN HOUSING

BY DR DINESH PALIPANA

Dinesh Palipana OAM is a doctor, lawyer, and disability advocate committed to building a more inclusive healthcare and disability sector. After sustaining a spinal cord injury during medical school, he became Queensland's first quadriplegic medical intern and now works in the emergency department at Gold Coast University Hospital. Dinesh is a senior lecturer, spinal cord injury researcher, and advisor to multiple national disability initiatives. His work continues to shape policy, research, and practice across the NDIS and healthcare landscapes.

A former senior advisor to the Disability Royal Commission, Dinesh is also a John Monash Scholar and Queensland Australian of the Year for 2021. His memoir *Stronger* was published in 2022.

• • •

CONNECT WITH DINESH AT:
WEBSITE: palipana.com
LINKED IN: @dineshpalipana

A Home Is Where Life Begins

Housing isn't just about shelter. It's not just having a roof over your head or ticking a box for compliance. Housing is where life happens. It's where everything starts: your health, your sense of safety, your connection to others, your ability to thrive. For people with disabilities, the right kind of housing doesn't just support these things; it makes them possible.

When we talk about Specialist Disability Accommodation, or SDA, we can't reduce it to a construction project. It's not just buildings. It has to be about creating homes that give people the foundation to access the rest of their lives. That means homes that support work, connection, community, and wellbeing. Homes where people feel like they belong, not like they're being managed.

I was born in Sri Lanka. I've seen poverty close up. I've seen people with disabilities sleeping on the street, dragging themselves across the ground without even a wheelchair. That kind of image stays with you. It shifts your whole perspective. It makes you understand that housing isn't just infrastructure; it's a human right. And it's something too many people still don't have.

After my accident, I had to relearn how to live in my own body. That also meant learning how to live in the world again through spaces, through design, through function. Every part of my home became part of my independence, from doorways to bathrooms to the way I accessed my wardrobe.

A home can either support or restrict your life. That's what makes SDA important. It's one of the few parts of the system that recognises the role of design in disability. It creates housing that's intentionally accessible, not retrofitted or halfway there. It gives people a chance to live with autonomy.

You don't have to wait for someone to help you turn on a light. You don't have to struggle to reach a cupboard. These things matter. They shape how you feel in your own skin.

When a home is set up right, it has a ripple effect. You eat better. You sleep better. You move more. You connect with others. You can go out into the world and focus on work or study, or community, not just survival. That's why SDA needs to be more than compliant; it has to be considered. It has to be designed with the person, not just for them.

In medicine, I see the consequences when housing falls short. People get sick more often. They stay in hospital longer. They rely on support workers more than they need to. Poor housing creates unnecessary barriers. But when a home meets someone's needs, you see independence. You see confidence. You see someone taking charge of their life again.

It's also about connection. A home should be a place where you feel safe and where you can build relationships. That could mean raising a family, having friends over, or just knowing you have a place in the world that's yours. That kind of stability can't be underestimated.

There are still too many providers designing houses that look good on paper but don't work for the person living in them, SDA homes that meet the standard, but miss the point. We need to change that because a home that doesn't feel like home is just another obstacle.

Getting housing right is the first step. Without it, everything else becomes harder. With it, everything else becomes possible.

When Housing Falls Short

I've seen SDA developments that technically comply with the guidelines, but if you walk through them, you can tell they weren't built for people. The layouts don't work. The materials are cheap. The spaces feel clinical or just awkward. There's no warmth. No thoughtfulness. Just compliance.

SDA is supposed to be a way to create homes that truly support people with disability. But in some cases, it's turned into an investment product that treats homes like assets on a spreadsheet. You hear a lot of talk in the sector about return on investment, but not nearly enough about quality of life. That imbalance is part of the problem.

I understand the role that private investment plays. It's critical. These homes don't build themselves. Capital is needed. But if the goal becomes profit over purpose, you lose the heart of it. You start seeing providers cut corners on design. You start seeing houses that look fine on paper but don't function for the people who live there.

I've been in SDA homes where, yes, they meet the guidelines, but they're hard to live in. Maybe the bathroom is accessible, but the kitchen isn't usable. Or the doorways are wide enough, but the turning space in the lounge is too tight. Or the place is so sterile and isolated that no one feels at home. Compliance isn't enough. It needs to be about usability. It needs to feel human.

When homes are built without considering long-term livability, you're putting people into spaces where they're stuck. It's not temporary; these are people's lives. Their everyday routines. Their health. Their sense of safety and comfort. It's not just a bad design decision; it's a failure to uphold someone's dignity.

The moment housing becomes just another income stream, we lose sight of the people we're supposed to be building for. That shows up in the lived experience of residents—in how easy it is to move around, whether they can cook their own meals, and whether they feel proud to invite people into their space. These aren't luxuries; they're indicators of whether someone can live well.

There are great providers out there who care about participants, who want to do it right. But others see an opportunity and forget that it's someone's home on the other side of that investment.

That's where we need to be clear. It's not wrong for SDA to be financially sustainable. In fact, it needs to be. But financial sustainability shouldn't come at the cost of human well-being. There's a middle ground. Some investors want to put their money into something meaningful, who want to be part of a social good and still get a stable return. We need to make room for that type of thinking and push out the kind that treats SDA as just another asset class.

We need accountability because once a house is built and someone moves in, it's hard to undo bad decisions. There needs to be more scrutiny, more transparency, and more willingness to ask: 'Does this actually work for the person living here?'

It's not complicated; it just takes the right intent. When you start with the question, 'Would I want to live here?' the rest becomes clear.

The Power of Integration

Technology has been incredible in my own life. My work as a doctor has allowed me to bridge some of the physical gaps

I face. It's helped me extend myself in ways that would have been impossible otherwise. That's why I believe it plays such a big role in disability housing. It can open options that weren't available before.

For someone living with disability, technology can change how you experience your home. It's not just about making life easier, although it does that too. It's about helping people live more independently. Whether it's lighting you can control with your voice, kitchens that move up and down, or doors you can open with a single thought, these things can reduce the need for constant support. That builds freedom. It builds confidence.

The pace of this technology is fast. What we're researching now with spinal cord injury recovery—things like thought control—will eventually flow into everyday life. If you can use your mind to control devices in a hospital or lab setting, why not use it to turn on your lights or adjust your blinds at home? These ideas aren't that far off. Some are already happening.

It's not just high-end innovation, either. I've seen how small changes in the home can reduce support hours, improve quality of life, and give people a sense of control again. You don't need complex systems; you just need homes that are set up to make those small wins possible.

This is where programs like Able Digital Wellness come in. Scott, who introduced us, is doing some interesting work in this space. They're looking at how to use apps and simple tech tools to help people exercise, eat well, and manage their health from home. It might sound basic, but when you have a life expectancy gap for people with disability, these basics matter. They're the difference between getting through the day and actually living well.

We still focus too much on diagnosis and what someone can't do, instead of looking at the body as a whole. We forget that everyone, regardless of disability, needs to move, eat, rest, and feel safe. These are the fundamentals of health. They're also the fundamentals of a good home.

Wellness programs and technology should be part of how we think about SDA because we're not just building accessible spaces; we're creating environments where people can build routines, take care of their bodies, and enjoy their lives. It's about independence, health, and connection, not just architecture.

But we can't rush ahead before getting the basics right. There's no point adding smart kitchens if the house itself isn't livable. If the provider doesn't care about the person. If the layout is wrong. If the human rights side of it hasn't been sorted. Technology should support a well-built foundation, not cover up poor design.

We need people who can see past the short-term. People who are willing to think about what this could look like in 10 years, not just what's profitable this quarter. That includes not just investors, but politicians, policymakers, and everyone in the system.

We're still working on getting that mindset in place. There are some good things happening already, but it's still in pieces. Some researchers are working with providers. Some clinicians are involved in design, but it's not fully connected yet. It's not a mature ecosystem. We need to bring that together.

We also need to clarify the roles within that system. A good example is support workers. There's uncertainty around how their work overlaps with clinical care. That affects how homes are staffed and how services are delivered. We need to define that better if we want to build housing that supports the whole picture.

The NDIS is still a young scheme—just over 10 years old. Compare that with Medicare, which has had decades to evolve. These things take time, but if we keep bringing people together and focus on the fundamentals, we can build something really strong.

Housing, health, and technology aren't separate things; they all impact each other. If we treat the home as the base for everything, as the place where life starts, we can make better decisions. We can design homes that help people live better, not just meet compliance.

Building with Intention

When we talk about disability housing, we need to remember that we're not just building places to live. We're building environments that shape someone's quality of life. That's why intention matters.

I really wish we didn't have to ask questions like, 'What happens when a home is built without thinking about the person living in it?' That should never happen. We're talking about another human being, someone who deserves safety, dignity, and a chance at a good life. These homes need to support that, not take away from it.

I've worked with the Disability Royal Commission, and I've seen what happens when systems fail people. There's still violence. There's still abuse and neglect in our sector. These aren't things from the past; they're still happening. They can happen in housing too, especially when providers aren't held accountable. That's why we need strong systems and strong policy settings to protect people from harm.

When we talk about policy, it comes down to two things: good incentives and real consequences. We need to reward the people who are doing the right thing; the providers who put participants first. The investors who want to build something meaningful. At the same time, action needs to be taken against those who don't. When the system allows poor behaviour to continue, it sends the message that it's acceptable. And that's not good enough.

This isn't just about business; it's about public trust. Taxpayers are funding the NDIS. People in the community expect that these homes are going to be safe, accessible, and fair. That they'll help people with disability live better lives. If that trust breaks down, it's not just participants who lose. We all do.

We also need to support long-term thinking. There's still too much focus on short-term returns, on ticking boxes, on getting homes filled. But this isn't a short-term issue; it's something that affects someone's day-to-day life for years. Maybe even decades. We have to look at housing through that lens. What's going to help someone not just survive, but live well over time?

That includes making sure we have the right people involved in the system. Not just capital investors, but also clinicians, architects, occupational therapists, designers, researchers, and people with lived experience. When you bring those voices together, you get better outcomes.

Right now, there are small collaborations happening. Some universities are working with providers. Some clinicians are involved in housing projects. But it's still scattered. We haven't built a consistent, connected system yet. That's what we need—a proper ecosystem that brings the right people to the table, with a shared goal of building something that works.

We need to be clear on who's responsible for what. Take support workers, for example. There's still confusion around how their roles overlap with clinical staff. That impacts how services are delivered and how safe the home environment really is. It's not a small thing. These grey areas can lead to gaps in care or even unsafe situations. That's why role clarity is so important in a housing context.

None of this is about adding complexity; it's about creating structure. If we want to future-proof SDA, we have to do it properly from the ground up. That means putting human rights at the centre. It means listening to the people who are living in these homes. It means designing with care, not just cost in mind.

We also need the political will to support this kind of long-term change, and I'm not sure we're there yet. Too often, decisions are made for short-term wins. But real systems change takes time. It takes vision. It takes people who are willing to build something they may never get credit for. That's what leadership looks like in this space.

The NDIS is still new; it's only a little over 10 years old. It's going to take time to mature. If we stay focused on the fundamentals. If we protect people, design homes that actually work, and bring the right people together, the future can be different.

But we have to do it with intention.

The Future I Hope to See

I hope that in 10 years' time, we've created a system where everyone benefits.

I hope people with disability have a great life and a home they can actually use. A home that's their base to go out into the world. A place that helps them access employment and education, where they can eat good food, pursue good health, exercise, and have good-quality in-home care.

I also hope it's a system where the economy and investors benefit as well. Where people can invest in something good, get a stable return, and feel good about what they've done for someone else. That's the kind of future I'd like to see.

If we can get the balance right, it's possible. If someone puts capital into housing that truly helps someone live a better life, and they also get a return on that investment, then that's the right thing. That's what this should be.

We can also use more innovation. We've got so much technology out there, and we've only scratched the surface of how it can be used. There are amazing ideas already in play. But we still need to get the fundamentals right.

Once we've done that, once we've made sure there are high-quality providers who care about participants and we've got all the human rights aspects properly sorted, then we can start to build on it. We can bring in more innovation, more ideas, and make it even better.

We're not there yet, and I don't know if we're going to get there. I've come to learn that the future is often out of our control. Things we think are going to happen sometimes don't. So I don't know, but I hope so.

It takes people who can see past short-term goals. It takes people who can think long-term. Not just people putting in capital, but also the politicians, the decision-makers, and everyone else involved. This is something that will take years to get right.

We're still figuring it out, but there's so much potential. There are people doing good work already. Like the work Scott is doing with Abel Digital Wellness. That's a good example of using technology in a way that really supports people. There's so much of that around—so many ideas that could make a real difference.

But we've got to get the base right first. Without that, nothing else works. And we need to make sure the people who are doing good work are supported, and the ones who aren't doing the right thing are held accountable.

This is a person's home; it's not just a house. That home can have an impact on everything else. If we can enable someone to live their best life, it doesn't just help them; it helps all of us. It helps the whole community.

It comes back to two things. One, this is a person's home, and it's a lot more than a house. Two, it needs to make sense for the people building it, so we can keep creating more of them. Hopefully, we keep looking at innovation and ways to make it better.

CHAPTER 3

DESIGNING SDA THAT GETS BUILT

BY KEIRA NICHOLSON

Keira Nicholson is a registered building designer, LHA and LHA NCC assessor, and a strong advocate for accessibility, inclusion, and sustainable living. As founder of Collective Design Agency, Keira combines professional expertise with lived experience of visible and invisible disabilities, bringing a personal understanding of how environments shape lives.

Her holistic approach weaves together sensory awareness, emotional well-being, and community connection to create spaces that feel safe, supportive, and truly like home.

Keira's work spans residential, medical, and public projects, always prioritising people over policy with care, dignity, and long-term functionality at heart. She also champions reimagining Specialist Disability Accommodation, pushing for housing that supports individuality, families, and lasting solutions beyond limited funding models.

• • •

CONNECT WITH KEIRA AT:
WEBSITE: collectivedesignagency.com.au
LINKED IN: @keira-nicholson-435929126

Designing for Real Life, Not Just Compliance

When Specialist Disability Accommodation was introduced, it was meant to create real housing options. Not just places to live, but places where people could feel safe, supported, and independent. But somewhere along the way, the purpose shifted. A lot of what we see now has moved away from people-first design. Instead, it's driven by what's fundable, what meets the standards, and what fits on a block.

We've been into houses that are fully compliant on paper. The plans tick all the boxes. The bedrooms meet minimum size, the turning circles are drawn in, and the layouts technically work. But once a participant moves in and you put a bed, hoist, storage, and assistive tech in the space, it becomes unworkable. Support workers can't move around the bed. Transfer paths are blocked. Storage is shoved in awkward corners. The house was built to meet a rule, not to support a person's life.

That's why we see SDA homes sitting empty. They pass the standard but fail the participant. And once a home is built that way, it's really hard to fix. The issues are in the bones of the house.

We've seen bathrooms where the turning circle meets code, but the placement of the basin and the way the door swings makes it impossible to transfer. Or kitchens where the appliances are technically accessible, but there's no room for support to be provided. It meets the standard but doesn't meet the need.

In living rooms, we often see the same thing. A space might be large enough on a plan, but once a couch and dining table are added, it's too tight. A participant using assistive tech can't get through without hitting things. If they need support with movement or meals, there's not enough space for another person to assist safely. These are everyday problems that make a home feel inaccessible even though it's supposedly accessible.

I always ask the same question when reviewing plans: would you live here? Would you feel good living in a home where everyone walking in the front door can see straight into your bedroom? Would you be comfortable bumping your chair around the furniture every time you want to get a glass of water? Because if the answer is no, it's probably not going to work for someone else either.

The truth is, a lot of SDA is being designed using standard housing templates. The minimum SDA guidelines get applied like a checklist, but no one stops to think about whether the house is actually liveable. That's what we see again and again, homes designed to tick the funding boxes, but not to support day-to-day living.

We also need to recognise that not all participants in an SDA require the same support. One participant might need quiet and space to regulate. Another might want to cook with support. Someone else might have visitors daily. When you design based on assumptions, you end up with one type of room for every person, and that doesn't support anyone well.

If someone spends most of their day in their bedroom, and that room is tucked into a corner with a restricted outlook or airflow, how does that support wellbeing? I've seen bedrooms with no desirable outlook, no courtyard access, and disconnected from the rest of the house. That wouldn't be acceptable in a standard home, so why is it considered fine in SDA?

We need to stop thinking of design as just ticking guidelines and start thinking about what people need in their daily life. The big question is: how will this space actually function when someone is living in it? That means considering the size and layout with furniture, equipment, and people included. Not just the empty room on a floor plan.

We ask things like:

- Can a support worker walk beside a participant using a hoist or wheelchair?

- Is there safe clearance for transfers?

- Can a participant prepare food with support, or will they always have to be a bystander?

- Can someone have friends or family over without being forced into shared spaces?

If those answers are no, then the house isn't doing its job. And once built, the problems become hard to fix and expensive to change.

What gets missed in all of this is that designing for real life is not complicated. It's just about asking the right questions at the beginning. Before plans are drawn. Before specs are signed off. Before the slab is poured. Because when you get it right early, everything else flows. When you leave it to the end, or treat it like a technical exercise, the outcome is a house that looks good in photos but doesn't support real people.

Lived Experience Leads to Better Design

I didn't come into this space through the design and construction industry only. I came in through my family.

My grandfather was like a father to me. He built his home and lived in it for 50 years. Later in life, he had a series of strokes. At first, he used a walking stick, then a wheelchair, and eventually, additional strokes caused paralysis and high physical support needs.

His home, the one he was so proud of, became a barrier. The hallway was too narrow. The bathroom couldn't be used. The whole layout had to be adjusted over and over. We tried to make it work by moving furniture, adapting routines, helping him manage. But a house can't be rebuilt without changing its bones. It wasn't designed to support the kind of care he needed.

He didn't complain, but you could see the impact. The frustration, the loss of independence. It was all there. It affected all of us. The constant reshuffling of the home, trying to find space for equipment, trying to give him some dignity. That experience changed the way I think about design. It made me focus on flexibility, on understanding how people actually use their space as their needs shift over time.

That's where my design practice comes from. Not from looking at the latest features or ticking compliance boxes, but from asking whether the house will still work five years from now. Will someone still feel safe, supported and comfortable when their mobility changes or when their care needs increase? If the home can't flex, it's not future-proof.

I also live with invisible disabilities. People often can't see them, but they shape everything I do. How I manage energy, how I respond to noise, how I experience light, materials, layout. I know what it feels like when an environment works against you. When it's hard to regulate or to find space that gives you calm.

Those things don't show up in the design guidelines, but they're just as important. When you live with access barriers every day, you start to notice the things that make or break a space. The way light bounces off surfaces, how noise travels between rooms, or how exhausting it can be to move through poorly planned layouts.

That's why lived experience matters. And why listening matters too.

There are a lot of homes being designed by people who haven't supported someone through complex care, or been in a space where assistive tech is being used. They haven't lived through the daily frustration that builds when a house just doesn't work. If you haven't lived it, then you have to be open to listening. Not just to tick a box, but to actually change how the design works.

We've been involved in projects where providers, participants and care teams were consulted early, and the outcomes were so much better. Simple things made a huge difference. Moving a bathroom door to improve privacy, creating a breakout space so someone could regulate without retreating to their bedroom, adjusting layouts so support workers had enough room to assist safely.

None of those things added cost. But they added value.

I always start with questions like:

- Who's going to live here?
- What kind of support model is in place?
- Will therapists or family be visiting regularly?
- Where will people go during a shift change?
- Is there space for quiet, for connection, for autonomy?

Those answers aren't in the guidelines. You find them by talking to people who live this every day.

You also have to go out to site. You can't design this kind of housing from behind a desk. You need to understand the land, the street, the community. Is there public transport? Are there footpaths? Can someone safely get to a café or park? What does a participant see when they wake up? A fence, a wall, or something that brings light and orientation?

Designing from lived experience isn't an extra layer. It's where good design starts. That's how you avoid mistakes, how you create homes that don't just meet the standard but actually support someone's life.

Plan Early, Collaborate Always

People come to us all the time asking for a quick concept. They want to go straight to documentation so they can submit something yesterday. We say no. Not until we've done our assessment.

Have you considered the SIL provider and the care model? Has a site been selected? What's nearby; any shops, transport, footpaths? Can emergency services access the site? Has an SDA builder provided a realistic cost budget? If not, it's too early to draw anything.

We've seen what happens when projects get rushed. When council and SDA guidelines aren't considered from the beginning, something always has to give. Usually, the design gets compromised, or the whole thing needs to be redone. And if the home gets built that way, it costs even more to fix.

One of the biggest issues we see is when design happens in silos. We have been brought in after to review concepts, the builder's been briefed, the consultants have priced everything. Then the council comes back with issues. Or the provider says the layout doesn't work. Or the care model shifts, and suddenly nothing fits anymore. At that point, it's not a tweak. It's a complete redesign.

We've had jobs where a simple planning overlay changed everything. Sometimes it's slope, sometimes it's bushfire risk, sometimes there are setbacks or heritage rules. If you don't know that up front, the whole project can stall. A planning officer isn't thinking about SDA standards. They're thinking about their local code. So when something like a wider driveway or hardstand area shows up on a plan and no one can explain why, they push back.

That's why the planning part can't come last. You need someone to check all of that before anyone gets too attached to a concept. A good SDA design starts with understanding the site, the local council, the care model, and who's going to live there. That's where we start every time.

You don't need a massive group of people to get it right. But you do need the right people. Someone who understands the planning. Someone who understands SDA and the care model. And someone who knows what day-to-day life looks like in these homes. That could be a support worker, a participant, or a provider; ideally all three.

These conversations don't need to take weeks. But they need to happen at the right time. Early.

We've worked on jobs where the support team gave small bits of feedback that changed everything. A hallway that looked wide enough on paper wasn't usable during care. A bathroom layout didn't work once hoists and personal care equipment were factored in. These aren't luxury changes. They're essential. And they usually cost nothing if picked up at the right time.

This is especially important when there's more than one participant. If there are two or three people living in a house, and you haven't thought about how they interact, what their needs are, or how support is being delivered, then you're working off assumptions. And assumptions get people stuck. One participant might need privacy and quiet. Another might need support to prepare meals in the kitchen. If there's only one shared living space, someone's going to lose.

We've seen houses where the living space is technically big enough, but once you put in furniture and equipment, it's hard to move through. There's nowhere for a family member to sit if they visit. There's no spot for a support worker to assist safely. Or worse, the layout creates tension between participants because there's no option to regulate and destress. That's when you see breakdowns, not because people are difficult, but because the environment isn't doing its job.

That's why collaboration matters. Not because it ticks a box, but because it picks up things that would otherwise be missed. We're not just talking about architectural flow. We're talking about real people and how they live, how care is delivered, and how homes function under pressure.

Designing from the start with the right people makes a huge difference. It's what stops the project from falling apart when something changes. It's what keeps the design aligned with how people actually live. That includes planning overlays, providers, transport, council, and community access. It all plays a part.

Every time we've seen a project fall over, it's because someone tried to do it fast, or alone, or without understanding SDA from the ground up. It costs more to fix it later. And the highest price paid is the family or participant who ends up living there or needs to pick up their life and choose somewhere else to live.

Homes That Work in Daily Life

We're often designing homes for people who will spend most of their time there. That means the space needs to work every day. It's not about what fits on a plan. It's about how people live.

If someone spends most of their time in their bedroom, that room needs to be the best in the house. It needs natural light, airflow, enough space for equipment and support, and access to other parts of the home. I've seen designs where bedrooms are stuck in dark corners with poor outlook and no way to access a courtyard. That wouldn't be okay in any other home, so why is it okay here?

A bedroom isn't just for sleeping. It's a place to recover, to rest, to regulate, and to feel safe. When you're tired, in pain, or overstimulated, that's the space you retreat to. It needs to support that, not just meet a measurement.

We see a lot of houses where the living area technically meets the dimensions on the plan. But once you put a dining table, a couch, assistive tech, and support staff in there, it doesn't function. Participants can't move freely, support workers can't help safely, and family members have nowhere to sit when they visit. It's meant to be a shared space, but instead it becomes restricted and uncomfortable.

Sometimes a design meets the SDA guidelines on paper, but fails in real life. The turning circle might be there, but the basin is in the wrong spot. The ensuite looks okay until the hoist goes in. The door swing might block the transfer path. These things pass in documentation, but when you're using the space day-to-day, they fall apart.

Tunnel homes are a good example. They're narrow houses with a long corridor, bedrooms on either side, and the living space at the back. It looks efficient on paper, but what you get is a clear view from the front door into someone's private bedroom. In a shared home, where people often don't know each other, that's a big issue. There's no privacy, and that affects how people feel about their space.

We're not building dorm rooms. These are people's homes.

When support workers leave bedroom doors open for ventilation or ease of care, everything becomes visible. Every visitor, every care team member, every housemate can see straight in. That's not okay. It doesn't give anyone the dignity or privacy they need.

In family homes, we make sure there's more than one living area. We create break-out spaces, spots to decompress, places to be alone. In SDA homes, we should be doing the same. If the environment is too noisy, too exposed, or there's nowhere else to go, people will retreat to their bedrooms and disconnect. Or they'll stay in the shared space and become overwhelmed. That's when escalation happens. Not because people are difficult, but because their needs aren't supported.

Participants don't all want the same thing. One person might need quiet. Another might need stimulation. One might want help cooking in the kitchen. Another might need space away from the group. If there's only one common area, it's not going to work for everyone.

That's why we ask basic questions when we design. Can someone close their door when they want privacy? Can they sit somewhere other than their bed if they're not up for socialising? Can a support worker do their job without being in the participant's space the whole time?

These aren't extras. These are the things that make a home liveable.

Support staff also need to work safely. If there's no room to assist with transfers, or no storage for equipment, they're working around obstacles every day. That affects their safety, too. We've been into homes where just adding one more storage cupboard or moving a doorway would've made all the difference. But no one thought about how the space would actually be used.

Outdoor space is usually the last thing people think about, but it really matters. If someone can't access their front yard or has no safe path to the letterbox, that's a problem. We've visited sites that looked great in photos, but in person the driveway was steep and there was no kerb cut. Technically it was accessible. Practically, it was a hazard.

Participants need access to the outdoors for mental health, for connection, for independence. A covered alfresco area, raised garden beds, space to sit with family or friends, these aren't luxury items. They're what make the space usable all year round.

Daily life is made up of small things. Moving between rooms. Sharing a meal. Hosting visitors. Having privacy when you need it. Design has to support all of that. Because if it doesn't work for how someone actually lives, it doesn't matter how compliant it is.

Building SDA That Lasts

We do not design for right now. We design for what happens next, next year, five years from now, when someone's needs shift or a care model changes. SDA is meant to provide long-term housing, not short-term fixes.

But we still see houses being designed so tightly around funding or one specific participant that they cannot flex when something changes. Then people move out or providers change and suddenly the house does not work anymore. That is when it becomes a vacancy risk. That is when a provider has to spend thousands to retrofit something that should have been planned from the beginning.

A future-ready SDA home does not mean bells and whistles. It means good planning, flexible layout, and the right structural allowances. Maybe that is hoist-ready ceiling to multiple areas, even if they are not used yet. Adding a second living space to a home with more than one bedroom means someone does not have to retreat to their bedrooms when they need quiet. Consider larger rooms for extra storage and circulation so equipment does not block pathways. These things are not upgrades. They are essentials when you look at how a home needs to work over time.

Some participants do not need physical support now but considering disability diversity we can design for it. I have had projects where participants have degenerative conditions. It is not about guessing the future. It is about allowing for it.

We also think a lot about Robust design. This is where people get it wrong. They go straight to stainless steel, bolted-down furniture, and anti-ligature fittings, and end up creating something that looks like a facility. We are not building detention centres. We are building homes.

I have worked on homes where we have used thoughtful material choices such as solid wall linings, secure cabinetry, and recessed fittings that still look soft and homely. You can still have warmth and texture and create a space that does not feel institutional. We look for ways to support behaviour and safety without stripping away all the personality of a home.

Durability and dignity can go together, but it takes more thought.

Another thing that gets missed is delivery. Some people think once the drawings are done, the job is over. That is when things start to fall apart. Drawings are only the beginning. If no one owns the approvals process or follows up with council, or checks compliance in early stages, plans won't meet compliance or enrollment.

We see it too often. Someone rushes to draw a house so they can say it is in the pipeline, but no one has checked if it fits on the block, or if the council will allow it, or if the care model is actually deliverable. Then it is back to the start and the timeline blows out.

We get involved in the delivery process because otherwise the design does not get built the way it was intended. If we are not in the room, details get missed. A builder might make a decision that looks small, like moving a wall without understanding the impacts, but suddenly a turning circle, and clearances no longer works. These are things that can derail an otherwise great project.

Assessors are not an end of project consultant, get them involved early, if they are not there can be large changes and delays impacting cost and delivery. These are avoidable if someone takes responsibility early.

A good design means nothing if it never gets built.

When we talk about SDA that lasts, we are not just talking about how long the materials hold up. We are talking about whether the space can change with the people who live there. Whether it can be used for different support models. Whether it still works if someone new moves in.

We have worked on homes where an extra living space changed everything. It allowed one participant to have visitors while another had quiet time. We have added covered alfresco areas that became the most used space in the house. Those changes are not expensive. They just take thought.

Flexibility is what keeps a house viable. That means future-proofing the layout, using robust but homely finishes, and leaving room for technology or care needs that might come later.

And most of all, it means asking, would I live here? Would I feel like I have control, space, and safety in this home?

Because if the answer is no, it is not ready for someone else to live in either.

PART 2

FROM PLANS TO PRACTICE

Making compliance
meaningful and delivery
sustainable.

'Knowing is not enough; we must apply.
Willing is not enough; we must do.'
–Johann Wolfgang von Goethe

CHAPTER 4

DESIGNING FOR DIGNITY

BY BRUCE BROMLEY

◌

Bruce Bromley is a nationally respected Specialist Disability Accommodation (SDA) consultant and accredited Disability Access Consultant, renowned for his strategic leadership and deep sector expertise.

As a co-author of the SDA Design Standard, Bruce has helped define the benchmarks for inclusive, high-quality and most importantly, desirable housing for people with disability across Australia. With extensive experience in SDA legislation, Universal Design, and neurodiverse-friendly environments, Bruce has shaped policy reform and operational strategy and has built environment outcomes that centre on dignity, autonomy, and accessibility. He provides specialist training in SDA and built environment compliance for people with disability, equipping providers, developers, and professionals to deliver housing that is not only compliant but genuinely inclusive and empowering.

• • •

CONNECT WITH BRUCE AT:
WEBSITE: sdaconsulting.com.au
LINKED IN: @brucebromley

Defining Dignity in Design

Most people take for granted their ability to live with privacy, control, and choice within their own home. This basic dignity in housing is something not afforded to many people with disability due to a seemingly simple concept—poor design decisions in disability housing.

All too often, I have walked through Specialist Disability Accommodation (SDA) homes to find they took a standard home design and tried to adapt or retrofit it for accessibility suitable for SDA, with no real thought given to how the home will be used. On paper, the houses might tick the compliance boxes. In reality, they can be impractical and undignified.

Bathrooms are one of the clearest examples. I still see providers placing participants in homes with shared bathrooms. No one should have to share a bathroom with another adult in their own home unless it's their choice. This isn't just a matter of hygiene, but about having a private space, a fundamental part of dignity. If a design forces people to share, it strips away that right before they even move in.

Space in bedrooms is another issue that comes up time and again. Many designs for disability housing squeeze in as many rooms as possible, leaving people with little more than a box to sleep in. There is minimal circulation space, a limited area to store personal belongings, and no sense of ownership. A bedroom should feel like your own space, somewhere to retreat to and feel secure. When the space is too small, dignity is compromised.

The selection and placement of fittings and fixtures within homes can have a significant impact on liveability and independence. A badly positioned tap or a heavy door handle may not seem like an issue, but for someone with disability, using it every day can become frustrating or even unsafe. For example, the standards state that a kitchen or basin tap must extend to a minimum of 300 mm from the front of the fixture. We then see designers placing these to the side of the sink without consideration of the end user. What happens if that person has paralysis on the side of the body where the tap is placed? It becomes unusable.

For Robust SDA, selection is even more critical, as standard fittings and fixtures are not designed to address the behaviours of concern exhibited by participants. For example, standard accessible tapware should not be used in Robust homes as the handle can be easily snapped off and weaponised against staff. Yet I still shake my head when I see a project specification issued to us for assessment that includes anti-ligature fittings and fixtures that create an institutional feel.

We're not building a prison cell; we're building a home. It clearly shows that the development teams don't understand the needs of Robust participants. Instead, with thought and careful selection, it's possible to develop a bathroom that differs little from a standard one, while maintaining a homely, personal feel as opposed to an institutional one. The same principles apply to wall linings, doors, furniture, and windows. Robust design isn't about making everything indestructible; it's about choosing practical and comfortable elements that stand up to use.

The feeling of a home is just as important as the layout. Compliance alone will never create a sense of home. A building can comply with the standards and still feel like an institution. Long, narrow corridors, harsh lighting, or exposed sprinkler heads all contribute to a clinical environment. What matters is how people feel when they enter the front door.

Does the home feel warm and inviting? Would you be proud to live there? These are the questions SDA and SIL providers need to ask.

Shared living spaces also shape dignity. In group settings, people should have enough space to come together comfortably without feeling cramped or forced into constant interaction. At the same time, residents need to have the option of alternative areas where they can choose to have time to themselves or spend time with visitors. Dignity is not only about privacy but also about choice: the choice to socialise, the choice to rest, and the choice to host family and friends without disturbing housemates.

Too often, homes are designed with maximum yield in mind, with the focus on how many bedrooms can fit on the block instead of what will make the home desirable. That approach might get a provider through the build, but it creates long-term problems. Poorly designed homes are harder to fill, harder to manage, and more likely to lead to complaints. Participants now have a real choice in the market. They will move out of homes that don't respect or consider their independence.

I encourage providers to start with dignity as the design brief. Before budgets, before compliance, ask: 'How will this home give participants privacy, control, and independence?' That shift in priority changes the way architects and builders approach their work. It encourages Universal Design principles, critical co-design with participants, and attention to detail. When dignity is the driver, the result is not only a compliant home but a desirable one.

The difference is evident in the details: a private bathroom, a bedroom with enough room for storage and mobility, lighting that the participant can control, and kitchens that can be used independently. These things may not add much to the cost of the build, but they completely change the experience of the participants living there.

On the surface, designing for dignity may seem more expensive, but the long-term value is undeniable. A well-designed home is easier to fill, participants stay longer, and families feel more confident in the provider. Poor design, on the other hand, costs more in the long run because it creates vacancies and frequent turnover. In today's SDA market, desirability has become just as essential as compliance.

SDA success also depends on its location because this factor determines how well residents can maintain their independence and self-respect while building relationships within their community. The placement of SDA facilities must avoid remote neighbourhoods that lack access to fundamental community facilities. Residents need easy access to services like shopping centres, medical services, parks, libraries, and other facilities. The availability of public transportation near residents' homes enables them to participate in education, employment, access healthcare, and attend social activities without needing to rely on excessive assistance from support staff.

The placement of SDA facilities in active, inclusive communities enables residents to maintain their independence while reducing social isolation and upholding the fundamental NDIS principles of choice and control.

Dignity is not an extra. It's the foundation of good housing. Every design decision should be tested against it: does this protect privacy, increase control, and create real choice? If the answer is no, then it's not the right design. That's the standard we should hold ourselves to.

Compliance vs Human Experience

Providers regularly say, 'The home is compliant, so it must be fine.' While compliance is important, my involvement with writing the standards means I understand the level of detail required. Compliance is only a baseline, and the design standards are a bare minimum. A home can meet every technical requirement and still feel institutional, cold, or unsafe. Passing the final certification isn't a guarantee that people will feel at home there.

An essential component of compliance is measurements: the width of a doorway, the ramp gradient, and the turning circle in a bathroom. Yet these details don't indicate how the space will feel for the person living there. A corridor can be the correct width and still feel narrow if poorly lit. A bathroom can have the required clearances but lack privacy if two people are forced to share it. A lighting plan can meet the lux levels, but overwhelm someone with sensory sensitivity if the lights can't be adjusted. The difference between compliance and dignity is in the day-to-day experience.

One of the most significant risks in treating compliance as the primary focus is that the homes look like facilities. I've seen homes that feel like hospital wards, finishes chosen only for durability, or sprinkler systems and exit signs mounted in ways that dominate a ceiling. While technically correct, these issues create an atmosphere that feels managed rather than lived in. SDA should never replicate the institutional environments, which is the intent behind moving away from group homes to SDA.

This is why co-design is essential. When participants are part of the process, you see what compliance cannot capture. Someone might ask for a second living space so they can host their family without disturbing housemates. Another might explain how vital an accessible outdoor area is for their well-being. These perspectives are not listed in the standards, but they make the difference between a tolerated home and a valued home.

Universal Design principles are another way to bridge the gap. Universal Design goes beyond accessibility, with the goal of creating intuitive, flexible, and usable spaces for the broadest possible range of people. In the late 1990s, a group of architects, product designers, engineers, and environmental design researchers at North Carolina State University created seven principles to help designers make accessible and inclusive environments and products. The principles of Universal Design exist as fundamental guidelines and serve as tools to assess and enhance usability, flexibility, and accessibility in design. The following examples detail how they can be applied to Specialist Disability Accommodation.

Principal 1: Equitable Use

Housing design needs to deliver equal usability and dignity to all residents regardless of their abilities. The purpose of the shared areas should be to create well-designed spaces that function well for all users through accessible pathways without requiring alternate routes or separate access points.

Principal 2: Flexibility

The design needs to support various user needs through flexible functionality. The flexibility of the furniture layout, adjustable bench tops with multi-height work surfaces, and adaptable storage systems enables residents to create their preferred living environment.

Principal 3: Simplicity

The design elements must present straightforward and easy-to-understand instructions for users across all levels of cognitive ability and experience.

Clear navigation paths, touch-sensitive markers, and contrasting visual elements help people move around independently. Wherever possible, a clear line of sight should be established between the front and rear of the home.

Principal 4: Effective Communication

Essential information needs to be delivered via three communication channels: visual, auditory, and tactile. This system provides support to residents who have sensory disabilities and neurodevelopmental conditions. The application of Luminance Contrast principles will assist all occupants, not just people with vision impairments.

Principal 5: High Tolerance for Error

The design of SDA environments needs to incorporate safety features that protect users from accidents and their resulting consequences. The combination of rounded corners, slip-resistant flooring, and safe appliance placement creates a risk-free environment while maintaining visual appeal.

In environments where there may be behaviours of concern, design must also include the protection of staff from attack. This can be achieved by ensuring fittings and fixtures can't be weaponised, and providing alternate paths of egress and eliminating points of entrapment.

Principal 6: Minimal Effort Required

The design should allow participants to perform their tasks with minimal physical strain. The system includes automated doors, lever handles, and smart home technology, which decreases the need for physical effort. The provision of fully integrated hoisting systems allows participants to transfer from the bedroom to the bathroom, and, where possible, these should be recessed into the ceilings to reduce the clinical feel of the environment.

Principal 7: Suitable Space and Size for Use

The design needs to include sufficient areas for people to move their support equipment, personnel, and personal items. It should also include wide circulation paths, accessible bathroom facilities, and private spaces that maintain resident dignity during care activities.

This is achieved by making bedrooms larger than the minimum specification, providing adequate space for people who use motorised wheelchairs to manoeuvre, while reducing impact with walls, doors, and furniture.

Technology can close the gap in participant experience. While a home doesn't require automation for compliance, consider the independence a participant gains from voice-activated lighting, automated blinds, or the ability to open their front door without waiting for staff. That is dignity. It's also a matter of safety. In an emergency, those features can mean the difference between a participant acting independently or depending on others to come to their aid. Technology shouldn't be seen as an optional upgrade, but a practical enabler of independence.

It's also important to consider the business reality. Families and participants have more options now than they had in the past. They can compare homes online, view them in person, and see if a potential residence feels like a home or an institution. While a provider may meet compliance, the home they deliver could still fail to attract participants. On the other hand, a house designed with the focus on human experience will attract participants, reduce vacancies, and strengthen the reputation of the provider. Desirability is as important as compliance.

It's also important not to dismiss compliance. It protects minimum rights and requirements to ensure a consistent standard across the sector. However, we should never confuse minimum standards with best practice. Providers who only focus on the rulebook will remain behind those who focus on the quality of people's lives.

The question I ask providers is simple: 'Would you feel at home if you had to live here yourself?' Compliance might satisfy the regulator, but it's the human experience that decides whether a participant thrives.

Designing for Safety and Independence

Safety in SDA is non-negotiable, but it can't come at the expense of dignity. Too often, I see homes where safety measures make the place feel more like a hospital than a home. The Building Code of Australia (BCA) and Standards require fire systems, emergency plans, and structural robustness. However, these elements should be integrated into the building in such a way that they are almost invisible to the participants. A safe home that feels institutional has already failed its purpose.

Take fire safety as an example. The BCA requires measures such as compartmentation, exit signs, thermal detectors, and fire sprinklers. These features are essential but should be designed to blend into the environment or removed via alternative performance solutions where suitable. A ceiling covered in exposed sprinkler heads sends a message of control and surveillance, not comfort. Concealed systems provide the same level of protection while preserving a sense of homeliness. Careful consideration of placement and design costs nothing but significantly impacts the experience of the participants in the home.

Balancing Design, Technology and Participant Control

Reliance on Onsite Overnight Assistance (OOA) staff for basic daily tasks can significantly diminish a participant's independence. Many of these tasks, such as adjusting lighting, opening doors, or managing the environment, can be enabled through thoughtful design and the integration of assistive technologies. Applying Universal Design principles and incorporating home automation empowers residents to control their surroundings with ease, reducing dependence on support staff and enhancing dignity, autonomy, and quality of life. The impact of such technology cannot be overstated; it transforms passive care into active living.

In contrast, the OOA's role during emergencies, especially a fire, must be strictly limited to self-evacuation. Given how rapidly fire spreads, it's neither safe nor feasible for the OOA to assist residents during an evacuation. To support first responders, it's recommended that an emergency bag be kept near the front door containing a laminated floor plan that identifies each participant's location, along with Personal

Emergency Evacuation Plans (PEEPs) for every resident. This proactive measure ensures emergency services have immediate access to critical information, enabling a safe and informed response. This is why fire sprinklers must be provided within all categories of specialist disability accommodation, as they will either extinguish a fire or at least slow the spread and, most importantly, reduce the level of smoke and carbon dioxide, the real killer.

Independence is closely tied to dignity. A person who can't control their environment isn't truly independent. Privacy is part of this too. Many homes are developed in a manner where the participants have no personal control over lighting or heating within common areas, or even their own bedrooms, because staff manage all the switches. That approach strips away choice. It's essential to acknowledge that independence is built on small details, including the use of home automation to control lighting, curtains, HVAC, a bathroom with enough circulation space for safe transfers that includes a cupboard for personal items, a bedroom designed so that equipment fits without crowding the resident, and potentially the inclusion of a lounge suite for relaxation.

Shared settings, such as rooming houses, present challenges. When four or five people live together, design choices can either support independence or create constant friction. Infection control can also be problematic in rooming houses where staff access participants' bedrooms and bathrooms multiple times a day.

Bedrooms should be large enough to hold personal belongings and allow mobility, not just fit a bed. Shared living areas should be generous, with enough seating and clear zones for different activities. Breakout spaces where someone can find solace when they need it should also be included. Independence is not only about what someone can do for themselves, but also the ability to decide how much interaction they want.

Outdoor areas are another overlooked area. Too many homes treat outdoor space as an afterthought. The provision of a large roofed alfresco area with room for tables and chairs, and easy access for wheelchair users, can significantly improve the quality of living for participants. Including transparent roller blinds so the space can be used during winter, and adding a built-in barbecue and raised wheelchair-accessible garden beds will increase the area's use.

Access to fresh air and a private outdoor retreat is as important for many participants as indoor space. Outdoor space supports mental health, provides a safe outlet for stress, and creates opportunities for social connection. Designing a quality outdoor area isn't a luxury but part of creating a balanced, independent life.

Robust SDA design deserves special attention. Providers often assume 'robust' means indestructible. They specify heavy-duty finishes, bolted-down furniture, and hard surfaces throughout the home. This results in a space that feels more like a detention centre than a home. True robustness comes from choosing surfaces, fixtures, and finishes that withstand damaging behaviours while still providing the experience of a comfortable home. It also requires anticipating possible risks. For example, a poorly selected tap in a Robust bathroom can become a hazard should the extension handle be snapped off, while a better choice of fittings avoids the issue entirely. Robustness should never come at the expense of dignity.

Neurodiverse-friendly design is another area that has been ignored for too long. People with autism or sensory sensitivities require environments that reduce stress rather than amplify it. Harsh overhead lighting, noisy ventilation systems, hard surfaces or cluttered layouts can all overwhelm neurodiverse participants. A neurodiverse-friendly home uses soft, adjustable lighting, soothing materials, and calming textures. It provides quiet zones where someone can retreat, and clear, predictable layouts that reduce confusion. These design features support independence because they give people control over how they experience their surroundings.

I have also learned that designing for safety and independence requires listening to both participants and staff. A designer may see a corridor as wide enough for a wheelchair, but a support worker may point out that it's too narrow to provide safe assistance. Participants may explain that they need storage within arm's reach, not across the room. These are the insights that turn compliance into real usability. Consultation should never be tokenistic; it's part of designing homes that work.

When viewing a completed home, ask yourself, 'Does the home allow a resident to move freely and safely without constant staff intervention? Does it give them private spaces that feel secure? Does it support choice in how much they engage with others?' If the answer to any of these questions is no, then independence is compromised, and if independence is compromised, so too is dignity.

Safety and independence are not competing priorities. When they're correctly balanced, they reinforce each other. A safe home gives participants the confidence to act independently, and a home that supports independence reduces risks because residents are less reliant on others. The key is to design a home with both goals in mind from the inception.

Lessons and Vision for the Future

After decades of working in access and recently on SDA design, one lesson stands out above all others: we must move from designing for disability to designing for everyone. The industry still thinks too narrowly, as though compliance is enough and 'accessible housing' is a specialist product. Instead, the industry would benefit from adapting to the broader consideration that suitable housing for people with disability is suitable for everyone. For example, wider corridors make life easier for a parent pushing a pram. Lever handles help someone with arthritis. Good lighting and clear layouts make homes safer for older people. When we embrace Universal Design, we stop seeing disability as a special case and start creating housing that works for the whole community.

Another lesson is that SDA and Supported Independent Living (SIL) cannot be treated as separate conversations. The design of the home has a direct impact on how support is delivered. A well-designed home improves the effectiveness of staff and reduces stress. For example, adequate storage reduces clutter and trip hazards. A second living area allows participants to socialise without conflict. A participant's ability to use the kitchen effectively reduces dependency on staff. When homes are poorly designed, SIL providers must compensate with higher staffing levels and more intensive support, which is costly and unsustainable. Good housing reduces reliance on staff and makes independence attainable.

The culture of design must shift from compliance to desirability. In the past, providers could fill homes simply by meeting the minimum requirements. That time has passed. Participants and families now have options between homes and providers, and will select the homes that suit their needs while providing a pleasant environment. A house that looks and feels like an institution will be rejected in favour of one that is welcoming and dignified. Desirability is becoming the new competition in SDA. Providers who understand that they are in competition with other developers to create homes that are desirable for participants will succeed by attracting participants first. Those who ignore it will be left with vacancies.

Looking ahead, I want to see SDA create 'forever homes'. Too many homes are designed for a snapshot of a participant's current needs without considering how those needs may change. Young people may not need ceiling hoists today, but they might in the future.

Forever homes are designed with built-in adaptability. They anticipate the potential for change in support requirements over time, preventing people from having to move as their needs shift. Moving is disruptive and often traumatic; therefore, we should design homes that people can live in for the duration of their lives.

Another part of the future vision is creating homes people want, not homes they're forced to accept. That means paying attention to aesthetics as well as function. A house that looks like a suburban home, with warm finishes and thoughtful design, tells participants they belong in the community. It avoids the stigma of being marked as 'different'. Design should create pride. Participants should have the freedom to invite friends or family over without feeling shame that their home is somehow less than anyone else's.

Technology will play a larger role in the future, but it must be used wisely. Automation should be focused on independence and dignity, not gimmicks. Lighting, doors, blinds, and communication systems are all areas where technology makes life easier and safer. However, technology should always be tested against one question: 'Does it give the participant more control?' If it does, it belongs in the home. If it doesn't, it's just clutter and could create anxiety.

The most significant cultural shift we need is to make dignity the central measure of design. Not compliance, not financial return, not even efficiency. Dignity. Does the home provide privacy? Does it offer choice? Does it create a sense of control? If yes, the house will also meet compliance, attract participants, and stand the test of time. If the answers are no, the design has failed, no matter how many standards it meets.

I want investors, developers, designers and providers to start every project by asking participants what dignity looks like to them. Some will say it's privacy. Others will say it's the ability to cook for themselves or to invite family over. Those answers should shape the design brief. Dignity is personal but can be built into the environment when we listen carefully.

The SDA sector is still young, and mistakes have been made. Too many homes were built quickly, with the expected financial return as the priority, and ironically, many remain vacant. Yet the future is an opportunity to learn from those mistakes and raise the bar. We have the chance to create a generation of desirable, adaptable, and dignified housing. That is the vision I hold for the years ahead: homes that work for everyone, that participants choose with pride, and that last a lifetime, a forever home.

Building Forever Homes

The future of SDA isn't about building more homes that scrape over the line of compliance; it's about creating homes that are desirable, adaptable, and dignified. Too many properties are designed for the duration of a funding package, not a lifetime. They work for the participant today but not in 10 years' time, especially if they have a degenerative disability. That approach forces people to move when their needs change, which is disruptive, stressful, and often unnecessary.

The development of homes that will support people with disability throughout their lives requires designers to take a new approach to functional and desirable design. A successful SDA home serves more than basic compliance because it incorporates innovative features. The design enables future support needs while creating private areas and communal spaces and maintaining the resident's autonomy through dignified living conditions.

A home assessment should include three key factors: desirability, adaptability, and dignity. When the design doesn't meet these criteria, it has failed. The implementation of these principles creates business advantages that benefit both participants, developers, and investors. These homes result in long-term tenancy, minimal renovation expenses, and participant trust. The market competition demands that businesses enhance their reputations above all else.

Practical Steps Toward Forever Homes

For providers ready to make the shift, there are practical actions that can guide the way:

1. **Engage participants early.** Involve tenants before the build, not after. Their insights will change the design brief in ways compliance never will.

2. **Think long-term.** Picture this home 10 or 20 years from now. Could someone age in this place? Could it adapt to higher support needs?

3. **Invest in flexibility.** Larger bedrooms, reinforced ceiling structures throughout the home, and

adaptable bathrooms cost little to construct but save significant costs later.

4. **Balance private and shared spaces.** Every participant should have a private internal and external retreat outside their bedroom, while creating living areas supporting connection.

5. **For Robust builds**, choose Robust, homelike finishes. Durability and warmth can go hand in hand. Robust should never mean institutional.

6. **Audit against dignity.** At each stage of design, ask whether the decision protects privacy, enhances choice, or increases control. If it doesn't, reconsider it.

These steps aren't complicated, but they require a shift in mindset. Forever homes are the result of consistent, thoughtful decisions that respect participants and anticipate their future requirements.

The SDA sector is still young. Disappointingly, the greed of developers and owners, their focus on yield in lieu of dignity, means that homes were built quickly without any consideration of the residents. However, the next chapter can be different. We have the opportunity to raise the bar, to design housing that people with disability want, that participants choose with pride, and that lasts for a lifetime.

The future belongs to investors, developers and providers who design for dignity first, in consultation with the people who will live in them. Standards will change, technology will evolve, and funding models will be adjusted, but the fundamentals will remain the same: privacy, choice, and independence are what make a house a home. Build those in, and you'll be ready for whatever the future brings.

CHAPTER 5

NAVIGATING SDA STANDARDS

BY TANIA GOMEZ

Tania Gomez is a seasoned entrepreneur and certified auditor with a passion for empowering NDIS and education providers to navigate compliance with clarity and confidence. With nearly two decades of experience, she has founded and scaled four multi-million-dollar businesses, beginning her entrepreneurial journey at just 21. Her qualifications span education, disability, business, and regulatory compliance, giving her a rare, cross-sector lens that enables her to deliver strategic, tailored support to providers aiming for excellence.

Tania's consulting style is deeply practical and people-focused, rooted in her firsthand experience in both care and education settings. She combines sharp business acumen with a genuine drive to create meaningful, lasting impact in the NDIS space. Known for her holistic, innovation-led approach, Tania helps providers not just meet standards, but rise above them, building organisations that shine for their quality, culture, and contribution to community wellbeing.

• • •

CONNECT WITH TANIA AT:
WEBSITE: Taniagomez.com.au
LINKED IN: @tania-gomez-5441bb80

What SDA Requires

SDA isn't ordinary housing. It's a regulated service delivered within a complex framework of standards, expectations, and risks. If you're a registered SDA provider, you're not just managing a property. You're operating a housing service under the NDIS, and that comes with strict compliance obligations.

These responsibilities aren't optional. They sit at the core of your registration. If you overlook them, you're not just risking a failed audit. You may also be putting participants at risk and undermining the long-term stability of your business.

SDA homes are designed for people with high support needs or extreme functional impairment. Each home must meet the features required under its SDA design category, whether that's Improved Liveability, Fully Accessible, Robust, or High Physical Support and maintain those features throughout its use. Once a home is enrolled, it becomes part of the national NDIS infrastructure. That brings a level of accountability that goes well beyond standard real estate.

Too often, providers approach SDA as a property asset. In reality, it functions more like a human service. That means you need to apply the same thinking you would to any regulated program: clear policies, strong recordkeeping, transparent processes, and a clear line of sight to risk.

The compliance requirements themselves fall under Module 5 of the NDIS Practice Standards. While they're often read as a checklist, they are actually a set of integrated service obligations. They cover:

- How participant rights are explained and protected
- How conflicts of interest are identified and managed

- How tenancy agreements are written and reviewed
- How properties are enrolled and remain aligned with their design category
- How tenancy management is structured, including maintenance, privacy, rent, and access

You need to be able to clearly describe how your service meets each one, not just in theory but in practice. That means not only understanding your obligations but also documenting them in a way that stands up to external scrutiny.

A common trap is treating compliance as the goal. It's not. Compliance is the minimum. What you're aiming for is quality. That's when the home is actually maintained, participants understand what they've signed, and the systems are running smoothly long before an audit comes around. If you're in a constant cycle of last-minute fixes and policy reprints, you're managing backwards.

The most common issues during SDA audits aren't dramatic failures. They're simple things that haven't been embedded as systems. The property might have been enrolled to standard, but no one's checked it since. There's no maintenance schedule. Agreements are inconsistent across tenants. Emergency plans are out of date or vary between homes. Records are scattered. The line between the housing provider and the support provider is unclear. These aren't difficult to fix, but they won't fix themselves.

Getting this right isn't about complexity. It's about rhythm. You need recurring checks, documented processes, and a working knowledge of what's happening across your properties and agreements. A clear list of what's being maintained, what's been reviewed, and what needs to be updated is often the difference between passing an audit and risking a breach.

This chapter is for SDA housing providers. It's not about support work or care plans. It's about managing the bricks-and-mortar service: the property, the tenancy, the records, and the risk. We'll walk through what the standards mean in real terms, how to manage tenancy well, and how to build a system that keeps you compliant year-round. We'll also look at what leadership needs to focus on to make it all stick.

You don't need the perfect system. You need one that works, is easy to explain, and keeps going.

Interpreting the Standards

The SDA standards in Module 5 may look straightforward on paper, but meeting them properly takes structure, planning, and clear systems. This section breaks down what each part of the standard actually means in practice. It's not about policy language. It's about what auditors are checking, what participants experience, and what you need to have in place to meet your obligations consistently.

1. Rights and Responsibilities

Tenants have legal rights. Your job as a provider is to make sure those rights are explained, upheld, and reflected in the way you manage housing. This includes offering information in plain language, explaining how concerns or complaints can be raised, protecting privacy in shared homes, and ensuring tenants know how to access their home and communal areas safely.

In practice, this looks like tenancy welcome packs with clear, easy-to-understand information; emergency contact numbers displayed in homes; simple complaint processes that are accessible to all tenants; and maintenance procedures that respect privacy. These aren't just nice to have, they're expected and essential.

2. Conflict of Interest

If your organisation provides both housing and support, you must show how those two roles are kept separate. Participants must be free to choose or change their support provider without pressure or impact on their housing.

You'll need procedures that clearly explain how this conflict is identified and managed. In daily operations, this often means having different teams for tenancy and care, making sure service agreements separate support and housing roles, and communicating to tenants that their choice of support provider won't affect their home.

3. Service Agreements

Every tenant must have a written service agreement that outlines both your responsibilities and theirs. These documents need to be easy to read, accessible, and aligned with SDA rules.

Effective agreements use plain English. They include details about the SDA design category and features of the home, rent and payment arrangements, maintenance responsibilities, access rights, and how the tenancy can be changed or ended. Strong practice includes consistent templates across all tenants, securely stored signed copies, and a system for tracking review dates. Tenants should be supported to understand what they are signing, especially where communication support is needed.

4. Enrolment of SDA Properties

An SDA property must continue to meet the design category it was enrolled under, throughout the life of the tenancy. It's not a one-time requirement. The structure, safety features, and accessibility elements all need to remain in place and functional.

This means you need to know what the enrolled category is and what features were included – things like step-free access, widened doorways, or assistive technology. You should log and assess any repairs or modifications, conduct regular checks, and keep documentation to confirm continued compliance. Contractors or staff working on the property also need to understand the importance of these features.

5. Tenancy Management

Managing an SDA tenancy goes well beyond rent collection. You're responsible for systems that protect tenant rights, support quality of life, and ensure compliance.

You need fair and transparent rent processes, proper notice periods for property access or changes, a reliable maintenance system, and secure recordkeeping. Staff handling tenancy management should be trained and able to manage these processes professionally. Good tenancy management shows up in written records of communication, complaints, repairs, and agreements that are up to date and clearly documented.

Compliance vs. Quality

Meeting the standard isn't the end goal, it's the start. Real quality comes from building systems that make meeting the standard easy and repeatable. When providers only think about these things before audit, they're reacting. When systems are built with quality in mind, you're audit-ready all year round.

Start with what you can control. Make sure your agreements are consistent and reviewed regularly. Set a realistic inspection and maintenance schedule. Be clear with tenants about their rights. Log issues, and follow up when they're raised. Small actions, done consistently, make the biggest difference.

Getting the Property Right

When a participant moves into an SDA home, they're relying on more than just a roof over their head. The home itself is the service. If the property no longer meets its enrolled design category, it's not compliant. If your maintenance processes are patchy or reactive, the service is at risk.

Understand the Design Category

Every SDA property is enrolled under one of four design categories: Improved Liveability, Fully Accessible, Robust, or High Physical Support. Each category comes with a specific set of physical features. These might include step-free entries, reinforced walls, emergency power, or assistive technology.

You need to know what features each property in your portfolio is required to have. That includes:

- Keeping a copy of the SDA enrolment documents
- Creating a checklist of required features for each design category
- Conducting regular inspections to confirm those features are still present and functioning

- Reviewing any changes or upgrades and assessing their impact on compliance

If any feature is removed, damaged, or replaced, you must assess whether the property still meets its category requirements. That includes small changes like flooring replacements or adjustments to fixtures. These must not affect accessibility or safety.

Maintenance is Compliance

Too often, providers think maintenance is just a practical task. But within SDA, maintenance is a compliance issue. Meeting the standard on day one is not enough. You are responsible for maintaining the property throughout the tenancy.

Your systems should cover structural elements like ramps, railings, flooring, and doorways, along with functionality in areas like heating, cooling, and ventilation. Emergency systems such as smoke alarms and lighting, as well as assistive technology, must be regularly checked.

A strong maintenance system includes quarterly inspections, clear tracking of reported issues, and documentation of when and how they were resolved. This isn't just good practice – it's part of your legal obligations.

Plan for Wear and Change

Houses age. Participants' needs evolve. Technology improves. These changes are expected, but they can affect compliance if not managed properly.

You need a plan for how you'll assess the impact of changes such as a new tenant moving in with different support needs, a bathroom being renovated, or the installation of new assistive tech. Each time a change happens, you must ask: does the home still meet its SDA design category?

You also need to document that assessment, and update your records to reflect any modifications. This is especially important when contractors are involved, as they may not always understand SDA-specific requirements.

Know Your Properties

Whether you manage one home or a portfolio, someone in your organisation needs to know the detail of every SDA property. At any time, you should be able to answer:

- What design category is this home enrolled under?
- What features are required for that category?
- When was the last inspection?
- What were the most recent repairs or changes?
- Does the home still meet its design obligations?

If you don't know, or can't provide evidence, that's a risk. Auditors expect you to be across these details, and to be able to demonstrate them clearly.

Be Ready to Show It

In SDA, saying you've done something isn't enough. You need evidence. That includes:

- Completed inspection checklists
- Maintenance logs and repair documentation
- Before-and-after photos for upgrades
- Invoices or certificates for key systems
- Notes showing how and when features were reviewed

This doesn't need to be complicated. A simple shared folder with date-stamped records is often enough. But it does need to be consistent and easily accessible when requested.

SDA Audit Readiness

Many providers only think about audits every three years, when it's almost due. The response is usually reactive: digging out old policies, chasing missing documents, and scrambling to fill the gaps. But that approach adds stress and risk. A strong SDA provider treats audit not as an event, but as a reflection of their everyday systems.

Being audit-ready starts with changing the way you think about compliance. If your service is running well week to week, the audit becomes just another step – not a crisis.

Set the Cadence

Audit readiness doesn't mean doing everything all the time. It means building in regular, repeatable checks that keep your systems moving. You don't need a full-time compliance officer, but you do need structure.

Monthly tasks should include reviewing open maintenance issues, logging tenancy communications such as complaints and entry notices, checking rent payments, and walking through at least one property, even informally.

Quarterly, conduct formal inspections against SDA design features, review tenancy agreements for upcoming expiry, check emergency signage and equipment, and update your internal compliance checklist.

Annually, complete a full internal audit across all properties. Review your tenancy management processes

Tania Gomez

and templates, re-check the property against original enrolment documents, and refresh staff knowledge of SDA responsibilities.

If something breaks or a risk appears, don't wait for the next cycle. Respond straight away and log the action taken.

Know What Auditors Look For

Auditors aren't just reviewing policies on paper. They want to see evidence that your SDA service is stable, structured, and running in line with the standards.

Expect them to ask questions like:

- Can you show signed tenancy agreements for each participant?
- How do you know the home still matches its design category?
- What happens when a complaint or repair request is made?
- Who manages tenancy, and how are records kept?
- What's the process for inspections, emergencies, and documentation?

You should be able to respond with actual examples and up-to-date records. No one expects perfection, but they do expect clarity, consistency, and follow-through.

Build a Simple Internal Audit Process

You don't need complex systems to stay on top of quality. A straightforward internal checklist or tracker can be enough to test whether things are working.

Check each of your core areas:

- Does the property still meet its design category?
- Are agreements signed, stored, and up to date?
- Are maintenance issues logged and closed out?
- Are emergency plans current and visible in each home?
- Are rent records and entry notices complete and accessible?

Test your own records regularly. Choose one property and walk through the file as if you were the auditor. Look for gaps or confusion. Then fix them.

Track the Gaps

A gap doesn't mean failure. What matters is that you can identify it, respond, and record what you did.

Maybe an inspection was delayed. Maybe a complaint wasn't followed up. What auditors want to see is that you noticed, addressed it, and made improvements. If your maintenance system fell behind for a few months, show how you caught up and what changed.

Being honest about gaps and acting on them is a sign of strength, not weakness.

Link Quality to Daily Work

Audit readiness isn't a separate project. It should be built into the way you manage housing every day.

If you walk through a property, log it. If you approve a repair, update the record. If a tenant calls with an issue, document the response. Every small action builds your audit trail.

Assign responsibilities clearly so everyone knows what they're accountable for. Keep records consistent, even if they're simple. And check that tasks aren't just assigned – they're actually done.

Avoid the Last-Minute Rush

You should never be caught off guard by an audit date. Mark it in your calendar and work backwards. Set reminders 12, 6, and 3 months out.

Use that time to:

- Update any weak systems
- Catch up on overdue agreements or inspections
- Close out maintenance requests
- Test your processes and records

Leadership and Oversight

Strong SDA services begin with strong leadership. You can't delegate compliance and expect it to stick. If you're a director, owner, or key decision-maker in an SDA business, you need to be across how your service is operating, not just from a distance, but in practical, day-to-day terms.

This section focuses on what leadership needs to understand, oversee, and influence to keep the business running well and reduce compliance risk.

Know What You're Registered For

First, understand exactly what your registration covers. This includes knowing which SDA design categories you're approved to deliver, which properties are enrolled under which category, and when your registration expires. You should also know whether your current systems meet the expectations under Module 5 of the NDIS Practice Standards.

Leadership needs to be clear on the distinctions between SDA and SIL, between housing and support, and between what your organisation is responsible for and what it is not.

If someone asks how tenancy is managed, how you track design compliance, or what your role is in property operations, you need to be able to answer without hesitation.

Set the Standard

Culture flows from the top. If leadership only talks about occupancy and revenue, that's where the team's focus will land. But if you also talk about quality, design compliance, tenancy rights, and record-keeping, these priorities become part of daily practice.

Make it clear that quality matters. This includes setting expectations around property inspections, agreement reviews, complaints handling, and communication with tenants. But setting expectations isn't enough, you need to follow up. Ask for updates, review reports, and read inspection results. When staff know leadership is paying attention, they are more likely to keep things on track.

Assign the Right People

As your business grows, you won't be able to inspect every home or check every record yourself, but you still hold accountability. Delegate clearly and make sure the right people are responsible for the right tasks.

There should be named roles for tenancy management, maintenance coordination, inspections, and document control. Ensure tasks are not just assigned but actually being completed and reviewed. You don't need to micromanage, but you do need a system that functions and reports upwards.

Quality and compliance must be regular items on your leadership meeting agenda. If they're not discussed at that level, they're unlikely to stay visible across the organisation.

Stay Informed

SDA is a fast-evolving sector. Regulations change, pricing is updated, and audit frameworks shift. Someone in your leadership team needs to stay across these developments.

This could mean reading NDIS updates, attending SDA forums, joining sector networks, or running an annual internal review of your own processes. The goal isn't to chase every headline. It's to avoid surprises and keep your operations aligned with current expectations.

Staying informed is what helps you shift early, rather than playing catch-up after something goes wrong.

Own the Risk

Every SDA business carries risk. Properties can fall out of compliance. Tenancy disputes can arise. A poorly managed repair can trigger safety concerns or audit failure. That's why risk oversight must sit at the leadership level.

You don't need to be alarmist. You just need a simple, transparent way to track known risks, record decisions, and follow up on action. This might be a basic risk register, an action tracker, or a short review each quarter of what's changed and what needs attention.

Being proactive is what matters. If an issue is identified, show that it was escalated, resolved, and learned from. Auditors don't expect perfection, they expect responsibility.

Final Checks

Specialist Disability Accommodation is not just about property. It is a regulated housing service. Like any regulated service, SDA delivery requires structure, consistency, and accountability across every part of the business.

You do not need a perfect system to meet these expectations, but you do need a reliable one. You need a way to check what is working, identify what is not, and keep across your responsibilities before someone else points them out. These final checks are not just about compliance. They are the foundations of delivering quality housing under the NDIS.

1. Know Your Design Category and Stay Aligned

Every SDA property must continue to meet the design category it was enrolled under. This is not a one-off registration detail. It defines the features your property must have and retain for the duration of its use as SDA.

To stay aligned, you need a clear register of all enrolled properties, including their design category, address, and enrolment reference. Each category—Improved Liveability, Fully Accessible, Robust, or High Physical Support—has a set of required physical features. These may include things like step-free entry, reinforced walls, assistive technology, or emergency power.

Regular inspections should include a review of these features. If something is removed, damaged, or altered, you must assess whether that affects your compliance. Even small changes, such as painting over signage or replacing flooring, can impact accessibility or safety. You need to be able to show that each property still meets its design category on any given day.

2. Keep Tenancy Agreements Clear and Up to Date

Tenancy agreements are the foundation of trust between you and the participant. If they are vague, inconsistent, or out of date, they put your service at risk. Every agreement should include essential details: the provider's name, the SDA category of the property, rent and payment terms, responsibilities for maintenance, complaint processes, privacy expectations, and emergency procedures.

Participants must be supported to understand these agreements, particularly if they require communication assistance. Agreements should be reviewed annually or whenever there is a change in tenancy, household composition, or property features. Keep a log of when each agreement was signed, where it is stored, and when it is due for review. Auditors will expect this to be in order.

3. Track Maintenance in Real Time

Maintenance is one of the easiest areas to fall behind, and one of the most visible to tenants. When something breaks or becomes unsafe, the quality of the housing–and your compliance–can quickly decline.

Build a simple system for logging issues, including when they were raised, who responded, what was done, and whether the repair affected SDA features. This does not require expensive software. A shared spreadsheet or property logbook can work well if it is maintained regularly.

Make it a habit to check unresolved maintenance issues monthly. Include repairs in quarterly property inspections, not just in response to tenant complaints. Document all work completed, and where possible, keep photos or contractor reports. Schedule servicing for items like smoke alarms, HVAC systems, emergency lighting, or assistive technology. Proactive maintenance is a sign of a well-run housing service.

4. Be Audit-Ready All Year

Audit is not just a test of your paperwork. It is a reflection of how your systems operate day to day. If your records are well maintained, your team knows the process, and your reviews are up to date, then preparing for audit should be relatively straightforward.

The best way to stay audit-ready is to break up the work throughout the year. Set monthly, quarterly, and annual tasks. Assign responsibility for each one. Use a calendar to track deadlines, not just in the lead-up to an audit, but throughout the operating cycle. When you check your own files, ask yourself the same questions an auditor would. Does this tell the full story of the property and tenancy? Could someone unfamiliar with the file understand what happened and when?

Keep everything logged. Record each repair, communication, inspection, entry notice, and decision. These records become your audit evidence. If you build these habits into your normal operations, you will not be caught off guard when an audit is announced.

5. Lead with Intention

Compliance does not stick without leadership. It is not enough to delegate responsibilities and expect them to be carried out. Senior decision-makers in the business must be involved, visible, and accountable.

Leaders should review the SDA property register, attend service review meetings, read inspection outcomes, and ask questions about what is changing or where the risks lie. Internal audits should be reviewed at a leadership level. Compliance and quality should be standing items in operational discussions. If leaders do not ask about these things, they will fall down the list of priorities for the broader team.

Ultimately, maintaining a high-quality SDA service is not about reacting to issues or chasing paperwork before an audit. It is about embedding structure, building reliable systems, and maintaining a consistent rhythm that supports your obligations year-round.

Final Word

Running a Specialist Disability Accommodation service is not just about managing properties. It is about delivering a regulated housing service for people with high support needs. That responsibility comes with clear expectations and serious consequences if they are not met.

You do not need to overcomplicate your systems to meet those expectations. What matters is that your structure is clear, your records are reliable, and your leadership is engaged. Providers who focus on quality from the start are better positioned to meet compliance requirements, support tenants effectively, and avoid last-minute scrambles when audits approach.

To keep your service strong, focus on five essential areas. First, make sure every property still meets its enrolled design category and that those features are regularly inspected and maintained. Second, ensure tenancy agreements are clear, current, and easy for participants to understand. Third, stay on top of maintenance with a system that tracks what needs fixing, what has been resolved, and how it was done. Fourth, build regular checks into your calendar so that you are audit-ready all year, not just in the lead-up to a review. And finally, stay engaged at the leadership level. Quality starts at the top and flows through the rest of the organisation.

These are not extra tasks. They are the foundation of what SDA providers are meant to deliver. When these five areas are in place, you are not just compliant—you are running a service that is safer, more consistent, and more trustworthy for the people who rely on it every day.

That is the kind of SDA that lasts. That is the kind of SDA that delivers what the NDIS promised. And that is the kind of SDA every provider should aim to build.

CHAPTER 6

THE REALITIES OF BEING AN SDA PROVIDER

BY PERRY KLEPPE

○

The visionary force behind GR8 Disability Housing, Perry Kleppe has been immersed in the world of property and finance since the mid-1990s. With his trademark out-of-the-box thinking, care, and compassion, and his exceptional attention to detail, Perry has turned the humble property management services business he started several decades ago into the leading NDIS housing provider in Western Australia.

Perry remains deeply involved in every aspect of our business, from property management to personally welcoming participants into their life-changing 'new, forever home'. Their tears of joy motivate him to raise the bar in disability housing ever higher.

Crucial to Perry's success has been flipping the conventional development model on its head. Participant wellbeing, along with choice and control—the cornerstones of the NDIS—has been made the priority. This is closely followed by the requirements of the care provider so they can deliver efficient, effective, and safe care.

• • •

CONNECT WITH PERRY AT:
WEBSITE: gr8disabilityhousing.com.au
LINKED IN: @perry-kleppe-a665a714

From Property to Purpose

I was semi-retired when we got into SDA. Our background was in property. We worked across development, sales, and management. For years, we operated through the usual Western Australian market cycles. There were short bursts of growth during mining booms, followed by long periods of stagnation. That pattern takes a toll. Rents fall, vacancies increase, and investors start selling. When they leave, they take your management portfolio with them, and that impacts the business.

Around that time, I came across SDA. I started reading into it and looking at how the funding worked. From a distance, it looked like a more complex form of property management. It came with a higher level of oversight, but also with a stronger, long-term opportunity. I decided to put in an application to become a registered SDA provider. I didn't tell my business partners until it was approved. If nothing came of it, that was fine. But if it worked, we would be well-positioned.

Once the registration came through, we were in. We had no experience in disability, no network, and no clear strategy. But we had a functioning property business. That gave us a foundation to start from.

In the beginning, I treated it like another property model. Find suitable stock, match it with demand, and manage the outcomes. But it didn't take long to realise this was a very different space. The systems were familiar, but the people side was something else entirely.

In traditional property, you often sit in a thankless position. Owners expect more from you, tenants feel like you work for the owner, and you're stuck in between. In SDA, we saw something we hadn't seen before. When we handed over keys to one of our first participants, the family cried. That reaction caught me off guard. It wasn't about the bricks and mortar; it was about relief. This was the first time someone had delivered on what they'd been waiting for.

That changed our view of what we were doing. This wasn't just about getting houses tenanted; it was about giving people a safe, long-term home that worked for their needs. The relationship was different. The impact was visible. And we could see straight away that it mattered.

We didn't set out to build a purpose-driven business, but once we saw what was possible, we couldn't treat it like conventional property anymore. We still focus on strong operations, but the meaning behind the work became a big part of why we stayed.

The Learning Curve—What I Wish I'd Known

When we first entered SDA, we thought it would follow the logic of the broader property market. Build the right stock, get it certified, put it online, and participants would come. That's how it works in real estate. You run a home open, 20 people show up, and you choose the best fit.

SDA isn't like that. We found out quickly that there isn't a busload of participants waiting. There's no set formula to attract referrals. There are no standardised marketing channels that guarantee results. Every single property is a separate process with its own delays, relationships, and obstacles.

Early on, we made the mistake of taking on an eight-unit apartment project. It was already built, and we saw it as a fast way to get started. We negotiated away most of our fees just to secure the management rights. On paper, it looked viable. In practice, it was a poor fit. The building was filled with high-net-worth owner-occupiers, and integrating NDIS participants into that mix created immediate problems. Complaints started almost straight away. It wasn't sustainable, and we had to unwind it.

That experience forced us to look harder at what SDA really needed to work well. It wasn't just about the house or the certification; it was about where the house was located, who the neighbours were, what the community looked like, and how the design supported care delivery. That set the tone for everything we've done since.

The other big moment came when we attended the Developing Australian Communities Expo in 2021. At that point, we still felt like outsiders. We didn't come from disability. We weren't sure we belonged in the room. I remember saying to one of our team members, 'I think we're going to get found out here.' I thought we'd be exposed for not knowing enough.

But within an hour, it was clear we knew more than most of the providers around us. We had systems. We had a structured leasing model. We understood the compliance obligations. That was the turning point. From that moment, we decided to go all in.

Looking back, I'm glad we made the early mistakes. We learned fast, and we learned early. A lot of providers don't realise they're in trouble until two years down the track, when their houses are sitting vacant and their investors are asking questions. We got our reality check straight away, and it gave us the discipline to build properly from the ground up.

SDA rewards long-term thinking, but it punishes assumptions. You need to test everything. You need to plan for nothing going as planned. That's how we approach every property now. If we're not clear on the location, the support network, and the demand, we won't move forward, no matter how good the floor plan looks.

Busting the Myths

There are a lot of assumptions about SDA, and most of them are wrong. The biggest one is that providers are making huge profits. You hear it all the time: 'You must be killing it with those NDIS houses.' The truth is, it's a specialised, high-risk part of the property sector, and if you don't know what you're doing, it will cost you very quickly.

People think you get your registration and that's it—you're in business. Just build the houses, list them, and the participants will line up. That's not how it works. Registration is just a licence to operate. It doesn't guarantee demand. It doesn't mean you have networks or referrals. You still have to do the work, and most of that work is relational, not transactional.

There's also this belief that higher specifications automatically mean higher occupancy. That if you build something that meets the standards—and maybe goes a bit beyond—participants will naturally be drawn to it. That's partly true, but it's not enough. Design matters, but location matters more. So do the support teams. It's not so much the support coordination; it's the care workers and SIL providers' ability to hire and retain them in these locations. Support coordinators struggle to drag themselves away from their workstation and are often remote from their participant clients. So is the track record of the provider. We've seen beautifully designed homes sit empty for months because they're in the wrong suburb, or because there's no support coordination in the area to help facilitate placements.

The other myth is around leasing models. A lot of owners and investors don't understand how their SDA property is being operated. We're seeing a pattern emerge where some providers are creating long-term, flow-through leases that sit outside the Residential Tenancies Act. They do it to avoid having to run trust accounts or hold a real estate licence. On paper, it might look clean. But in practice, it removes important protections for both the participant and the investor.

In our business, we don't do that. All rent goes through a trust account. We operate under the correct legal structures and manage properties in accordance with the legislation in our state. That means we're audited. It means there's oversight. It also means we can demonstrate where every dollar has gone, which is important when something goes wrong.

This isn't a space where shortcuts pay off. Some providers have structured their whole model around front-end revenue. They get a payment when the property is built, and that's where their income stops. There's no plan for long-term management. No infrastructure. No service delivery. And once the market shifts or participant demand drops, those businesses collapse, and they leave owners with vacancies and no support.

If you're not building something sustainable, you're not building anything at all.

The Stakeholder Web—Managing Complex Relationships

SDA doesn't run on properties; it runs on people. And not just the participants. Every single house involves a network of stakeholders: support coordinators, SIL providers, families, investors, OTs, builders, and plan managers. If you don't manage those relationships well, it doesn't matter how good the house is. It won't work.

One of the first things we did was build a hierarchy of priorities. It guides how we make decisions. The participant comes first, always. Second is the care provider. If they can't deliver the supports safely and efficiently, everything falls apart. We put ourselves third, as the SDA provider. The investor is fourth. That might sound backwards to some people, but it's how we get long-term success. If we don't get the participant and the care provider aligned, the house won't remain stable. And if the house isn't stable, the investor won't see the returns they expected.

We've structured our team internally to reflect that complexity. I focus on the higher-level relationships: strategic conversations, partnerships, and governance. Stephanie manages onboarding for new collaborations. She's the point of contact for SILs and support coordinators. Tania looks after property onboarding and manages our investor relationships. Under Stephanie is our property management team, led by our agency, which handles day-to-day participant issues, maintenance, and compliance.

It's not about having a big team; it's about having the right structure so nothing falls through the cracks. Everyone needs to know who they're dealing with and what the process is. Otherwise, you're just adding confusion to an already complex system.

One of the most important things we do is hold group property viewings before any commitment is made. That's not just a walk-through. We bring in everyone involved: participant, family, support coordinator, SIL provider, sometimes even the OT. We want alignment right from the start. We want families to understand how the next participant will be selected, what the care model looks like, and what the house will look like once tenanted.

This helps manage expectations early. It also avoids the situation where someone commits to a house, only to find out later that it's not suitable for the care team, or that a family member isn't comfortable with the other tenants. Once someone moves in, it's much harder to fix those problems.

We also conduct quarterly inspections under the Residential Tenancies Act. That's about more than maintenance; it gives us visibility. We can pick up early signs of wear and tear, or potential issues with the care being delivered. We're not the compliance body, but we can't pretend we don't have a role in safeguarding quality.

Support coordinators and SIL providers are critical in all of this. They're often the main source of referrals, but they can also be the biggest barrier if the relationship isn't managed properly. That's why consistency matters. Our homes follow a standard design. Fire safety equipment is in the same place. Appliances are the same. The layout changes slightly, but the functionality doesn't. That means SILs can move their teams between houses easily. No retraining. No confusion.

We don't deal with architects; we deal with builders. We tell them what we want. If it doesn't match our model, we don't take it on. That might sound rigid, but we've found it's the only way to deliver a consistent outcome.

Managing relationships at this level is full-time work. But if you get it right, everything else becomes easier. And if you ignore it, you'll be chasing your tail from day one.

Playing the Long Game

In this line of work, you're assumed to be in the wrong until you can prove otherwise. That becomes obvious the first time something goes sideways and you're dealing with the Commission. If your systems are weak or your documentation isn't thorough, you'll struggle to defend your position. It doesn't matter how well-meaning you are. If it's not written down, it didn't happen.

We decided early on that compliance couldn't be treated as a once-a-year task. It had to be part of how we operated every week. So now, every week without fail, our entire team comes together to review complaints, maintenance issues, risks, and anything flagged for improvement. We don't wait until something escalates; we work through it while it's still manageable.

That approach paid off during our second audit. We didn't receive a single non-conformity. To be honest, we expected a few notes, probably around how we handled complaints or how we logged our follow-up actions. But the audit came and went with no issues raised. That didn't happen because we got lucky; it happened because we were prepared.

A big part of that came down to Lachlan. He joined us after our first audit and took the lead on compliance and quality systems. He's the type who will spend the weekend finding the answer to something if he doesn't know it by Friday. Twelve months out from our next audit, he started working through everything—policies, procedures, evidence. He made sure it was all up to date and that everyone in the business understood how it worked in practice.

A lot of providers don't approach it this way. They do what they need to do to get through registration, and then they put it on the shelf. That's a mistake. In SDA, things move. Regulations shift. Expectations change. You can't afford to let your systems sit still.

We saw just how important this was during a complaint process that went all the way to the Quality and Safeguards Commission. It involved a couple living in one of our early apartment projects. On the surface, things looked fine, but over time, the situation with their care provider became difficult. The provider started raising constant issues, many of them unfounded, and escalated them to anyone who would listen. Eventually, the complaint reached federal offices and triggered a formal investigation.

Because our systems were solid, we were able to demonstrate exactly what had taken place. Every conversation, every site inspection, every decision had been documented. We had a clear record. The Commission reviewed the case and found no issue with how we'd handled the situation. In the end, we helped the couple transition out of that apartment and into a better fit, but it could have gone very differently.

That experience confirmed for us what we already believed. If you want to operate in this space, you need the infrastructure, not just forms and templates, but real systems that are used daily and understood by everyone. Audits aren't the hard part. It's what you do between them that makes the difference.

You can't build compliance into the business at the last minute. If it isn't part of how you operate every week, you're leaving yourself open.

The Business–Participant Balance

A lot of providers try to separate the business side from the participant side. In our experience, that doesn't work. If your participants and care providers aren't stable, your business won't be either. Every vacancy, every poorly matched household, every churn in support teams costs time and money. We decided early on to build our model around stability first.

We take a participant-first approach, not because it sounds good, but because it works. If the person living in the home feels safe and supported, and their care team can deliver services properly, everything else holds. Investors are happy. The house stays full. There are fewer complaints. That's what long-term performance looks like in this sector.

One of the decisions we made was to never fill a house just to tick a box. If an investor has a two-bedroom property, we focus on getting the first participant placed and supported before we even look at the second room. We don't go chasing a quick second tenancy just to get a rent stream going. That doesn't help anyone if the participants aren't compatible.

It's not a high-volume model. It's not fast. But it works. We've had properties sit for six or seven months with only one tenant because we couldn't find the right second fit. It's frustrating for the investor in the short term, but in the long run, it delivers the outcome they actually want, which is a stable asset with minimal disruption.

We also try to make sure every investor in our portfolio has at least one participant placed before we go back to fill second bedrooms or shared tenancies. That's how we balance equity across the network. It's not about favouring certain people or properties; it's about making sure everyone gets traction before anyone gets ahead.

Most of the serious problems we've seen in other businesses have started with rushed placements. Someone moves in who isn't right for the house or the co-tenants, and before long, care providers start burning out, participants disengage, and eventually, someone exits. By then, the damage is done. Trust is lost. The house has a reputation, and it becomes harder to place the next person.

We built our systems to prevent that cycle. It means going slower at the front end, but it pays off. We've had investors come to us after working with other providers, saying they just want their house filled. Our answer is always the same— not at any cost.

Learning from Participants

When we first started, we would have taken anyone. If a participant expressed interest and met the funding criteria, we tried to make it work. That was the mindset—get people into homes, prove the model works, move things forward. We didn't have a framework for saying no.

Over time, we realised that not every participant is the right fit, and forcing it only causes problems later. These days, we run a structured application process. It's not about being exclusive; it's about being honest about what we can deliver.

One of the first filters we look at is compatibility. Can the person live with others? Do they want to? If someone needs to live alone but only has funding for a shared arrangement, it's not going to work. We won't try to make it work. That doesn't mean they won't find a suitable property elsewhere; it just means our model isn't the right fit.

It's hard to say no, especially when you know the person is struggling to find housing. But saying yes to the wrong placement helps no one. The participant ends up unhappy, the care team burns out, and the household breaks down. That creates more movement, more instability, and more pressure on the system.

We've also seen how important it is to be clear with families from the start. Some families come in with expectations that aren't aligned with how SDA operates. They might expect their loved one will live alone in a two-bedroom home or have full-time support on-site. If that's not supported by the plan or the funding, it's better to have that conversation upfront. It avoids conflict later.

When we do get the match right, you see it quickly. The household is calm. The support workers are consistent. The property is looked after. The participant feels at home. That's what we aim for every time.

We're not a placement agency; we're a housing provider. But if we ignore compatibility, we're not doing our job. The right match takes more time, but it saves everyone—participants, families, investors, and our own team—from unnecessary disruption.

We've learned to treat every placement like it matters, because it does.

Where the Sector is Headed

What we're seeing now in SDA reminds me of what happened in finance broking years ago. At the start, it was full of small, independent operators running their own models. Then the aggregators came in, the regulations tightened, and the sector consolidated.

The same thing is happening here. The providers who thought this would be easy money are starting to disappear. Some have already folded. Others are barely hanging on, relying on front-end project fees because they've got no long-term management plan in place. We've had investors come to us after their original provider went silent—no rent, no updates, no care for the property. That's where the damage starts.

This industry will tighten. Regulation is only going in one direction, and rightly so. Too many providers are still flying under the radar. Some don't use trust accounts. Some run lease structures that aren't legal. Some don't even have the right licences to manage real estate. It's not sustainable. And when participants get hurt, the sector bears the cost.

Over the next five years, we'll see a small group of national providers doing volume, a few strong state-based players, and a limited number of boutique providers that focus on a specific region or participant group. Everyone else will either be absorbed or exit. We've chosen to lean into that. Rather than trying to fight change, we're building a business that can handle it. That means tightening up our systems, investing in our people, and staying close to our referral networks.

It also means being visible. We're not hiding behind a website or waiting for referrals to come to us. We run information sessions. We speak at events. We invite families and support coordinators into our properties before anything is finalised. That visibility builds trust, and in a sector that's still finding its identity, trust is everything.

We also focus heavily on education. That's been one of our best tools, both for protecting the business and lifting the bar for the sector. We host events like the Building Better Business Breakfasts. They're not marketing exercises; they're forums to help SIL providers and support coordinators understand how this space actually works. We talk about legal obligations, risk, vacancy, and long-term sustainability; no sugar-coating.

That work doesn't give us an immediate return, but it positions us where we want to be—as a provider that's here for the long run, not just the initial build.

The days of quick wins in SDA are over. The future will belong to providers who take it seriously, do the work properly, and deliver consistently. Everyone else is on borrowed time.

Final Advice—For the Brave

Building Better Business Breakfast doesn't have any content for investors. It's targeted specifically at SIL providers and support coordinators and, as the name suggests, is education around ensuring you're doing the business well. That's just as important as the care delivery, the compassion, and empathy. If you drop the ball on doing the business well, all the compassion and empathy in the world won't help the provider (or more importantly, the participants) if they fail in the business area.

People still come to me thinking SDA is the next big thing. They've read the pricing guide, they've seen the returns on paper, and they want to know how to get started. My first thought is usually the same: I *think you've missed the boat.*

That's not because there's no opportunity left. There is. But it's harder now. It takes more than a clean design and a registration certificate. You need the right location, the right partners, and a business that can hold up under pressure. You also need to be prepared to wait. Returns don't happen overnight. Relationships take time to build. So do systems.

If you're still thinking about SDA like it's a property play, you'll struggle. This isn't about maximising rent; it's about getting someone into a home where they'll stay. That means you need to understand support networks, participant funding, and compatibility. You need to know what's happening in the local market, not just what's on the national roadmap.

This sector rewards consistency and trust. If you're not in it for the long term, don't start. Because the damage from a poorly run SDA property doesn't just hurt your business; it affects participants, families, and investors who believed they were getting something stable.

My advice is simple: focus on quality. Focus on people. Know your obligations. Build relationships before you build houses. And only step into this space if you're prepared to run it properly.

We didn't come into this with a big plan, but we built the business slowly, stayed close to what mattered, and made decisions based on what worked. That's what kept us here. If you're serious about SDA, that's the mindset you'll need.

PART 3

THE ROAD AHEAD—DEMAND, DATA, AND SYSTEM CHANGE

Looking at where SDA is heading and what must change to meet future needs.

'The best way to predict the future is to create it.'

—Peter Drucker

CHAPTER 7

SDA DEMAND AND DATA USING DATA TO DELIVER SMARTER SDA HOUSING

BY HONG KNOWLING

Hong is a property and planning professional with over 20 years of experience, specialising in disability-inclusive development, healthcare, childcare, seniors living, and other social infrastructure. With a strong command of property economics and demand dynamics, Hong blends strategic town planning insight with rigorous analysis to guide successful projects. In 2017, she founded PPC Urban (Planning Property Consultants) with a vision to help investors identify and deliver highly leasable and saleable assets by aligning market demand, investment risk, and government approval priorities.

Her expertise spans market feasibility, demographic assessment, infrastructure planning, investment strategy, and town planning approvals across Australia. Drawing on this breadth, Hong has delivered projects that balance social outcomes with strong commercial performance.

• • •

CONNECT WITH HONG AT:
WEBSITE: ppcurban.com.au
LINKED IN: @hong-knowling-3a17ba1b

Why SDA Needs Better Data

In the SDA market, everyone wants to talk about demand, but very few people are using the data properly. The result is a growing disconnect between what's being built and what's actually needed. This creates oversupply in some areas, persistent vacancies in others, and ultimately, poor outcomes for both investors and participants.

In the NDIS 2023 review, *Working Together to Deliver the NDIS*, the NDIS noted, among other things:

'*The SDA market is still maturing, but has achieved much to date, attracting a large amount of private investment and increasing the supply of specialist accommodation. Nevertheless, there is a mismatch in demand and supply. Utilisation of SDA funding is also low, and at the same time, many SDA dwellings sit vacant. As a result, the SDA market is not yet delivering the right homes in the right locations.*'

The root of the issue is that many people treat demand as a single headline number. They might quote the total number of NDIS participants or refer to state-wide SDA figures without asking the critical questions underneath. How many of those participants are SDA-funded locally? What design categories are they eligible for? Where do they want to live? Are there care services available in that area? These details matter. Without them, the data is meaningless.

This is why SDA development needs better data, or more accurately, better use of the data that already exists. The most authoritative source in this space is the NDIA itself. Every quarter, it publishes updated reports on SDA supply, demand, and housing goals. These datasets are transparent, public, and based on formal processes under the NDIS Rules. If you want a reliable baseline, this is where you start.

But even good data can be misused. Some investors still rely on anecdotal provider feedback as their primary source of demand insight. While providers can offer useful on-the-ground context, they're limited by what they see in their own portfolios. Their feedback is shaped by local experience and often reflects only part of the picture. We've seen cases where one provider claims there's unmet demand in a region, only for the data to show that supply is already saturated and more projects are in the pipeline.

This isn't to say local insight doesn't matter; it does. But it should always be used alongside hard data, not instead of it. Relying on a single data point, or one (or even more) provider's view, isn't a market assessment. It's an opinion. The most accurate view comes from combining verified SDA data, local demographics, care workforce capacity, and current planning activity.

Investors who skip this process are often the ones asking for quick answers. Some expect to be spoon-fed every piece of critical information without doing any of the due diligence themselves. But SDA investment doesn't work that way. It requires active investigation and interpretation. This is where expert analysis adds real value, not by handing over perfect answers, but by helping people ask the right questions and make informed, confident decisions.

If you want to avoid mismatched housing, long-term vacancies, and financial stress, you have to go beyond assumptions and start with evidence.

Trust the NDIS Data, But Know Its Limits

The NDIA publishes some of the most reliable and comprehensive data available in the SDA sector. It includes quarterly reports, detailed supply and demand dashboards, housing goal insights, and enrolment figures. These datasets form the foundation of any credible SDA market assessment.

Yes, you can trust this data, but like any dataset, it has limitations. It's not perfect, and it's not designed to do everything.

One of the most common questions I am asked is whether SDA data from the NDIA is out of date. Some people suggest it lags behind market activity by 6 to 12 months. That is not easy to verify, and could be true in isolated cases, but it's rarely significant.

Like many government agencies, the NDIS faces ongoing backlog issues due to limited staff and resources. The timing of how quickly this work is processed is uncertain and unlikely to be resolved soon. But it's important to remember that the SDA market moves slowly compared to mainstream real estate, where conditions can shift weekly. In SDA, even if the data is a quarter behind, the insights remain valid.

Another gap is the project pipeline. The NDIA tracks pipeline dwellings only once a building permit is issued. Anything before that, even if it's under design or planning, is invisible in the data. That means areas with significant upcoming supply might still appear to have a shortfall when, in fact, new stock is already on the way. You can only pick this up through planning intelligence or engagement with local councils.

Another limitation is that the data captures enrolled supply, not physical occupancy. This means a dwelling may be listed as available but not yet tenanted. It also doesn't track unfunded or pending participant applications, which could change the picture in some areas. Still, these gaps are relatively minor. The dataset is structured, consistent, and updated regularly. It's far more useful than most other sources available to the sector.

That said, the data doesn't assess commercial viability. It won't tell you whether a specific project makes financial sense. It doesn't model cash flow, expected lease-up time, or rental performance. It won't flag when a site might be unfeasible due to location rules or finance restrictions. That's the job of the investor or their advisor. This is where a lot of people go wrong. They treat raw data as if it answers every question, when, in fact, it just tells part of the story.

This is why due diligence matters. You need to layer data sources, check what's missing, and use context to interpret what the numbers mean.

The NDIA data is a strong foundation, but it's not a complete picture. Used properly, it can help identify risk, highlight opportunity, and guide smarter decisions, but only if you understand where its boundaries are.

What Drives SDA Demand

A lot of people assume SDA demand is simple. They look at the number of NDIS participants and conclude that demand must be high. But the reality is more complex. Total participant numbers mean very little on their own. Real demand depends on several interconnected factors, and unless you understand them properly, it's easy to misread the market.

The first and most critical filter is eligibility. Not all NDIS participants are eligible for SDA. In fact, only a small proportion qualify. Even among those who are eligible, not all have funding yet. Some are still going through assessments, while others are waiting for plan reviews. If you're looking at raw NDIS numbers without checking who is SDA-funded and seeking housing, you're already several steps removed from the truth.

Design category fit is the next layer. SDA demand isn't one market; it's made up of different categories: Improved Liveability, Fully Accessible, High Physical Support, and Robust. Each category has its own needs and challenges. You might see unmet demand in one and oversupply in another, all within the same region. It's the same with dwelling types. A participant might need a villa, not an apartment, or vice versa. If the product doesn't match the need, it won't lease, no matter how many eligible participants are in the area.

Location matters too. SDA demand is highly place-specific. Participants want to live near family, near their support networks, and near services they already know. Even within a city, demand can vary from one suburb to the next. A property that's 10 minutes too far from a person's preferred location might be completely unviable. This is something investors often overlook, especially when they rely on high-level averages or blanket assumptions about demand.

Support availability is another key factor. You can't run a successful SDA home without care staff. Even if the participant is funded, they need a provider who can deliver the right supports in the area. If the workforce isn't there, the home will remain vacant. We've seen this happen in regions where the housing looked viable on paper, but the provider couldn't staff it.

Policy settings also influence demand in a practical way. Pricing reviews, location rules, and design standard changes can impact what is built and where. Developers who don't keep track of these changes can find themselves stuck with a product that no longer meets the rules or the market.

Finally, we're seeing steady demand driven by the retirement of legacy stock. As older dwellings are phased out, more participants are being assessed for new housing. While this shift isn't always visible in the data, experienced specialists such as PPC Urban can interpret the signals and estimate the opportunities it creates. These insights are critical in shaping medium-term demand.

In short, SDA demand isn't one number; it's a set of conditions that all need to align. The biggest mistake I see is when investors focus only on participant totals or rely on a provider's opinion without checking the data.

To build a successful SDA project, you have to go deeper. Understand who is eligible. Know what they need. Make sure the local environment can support them. Most importantly, assessments must be carried out on a local scale, where real demand and context become visible.

The Danger of Headline Demand

One of the most common mistakes I see in the SDA sector is relying on headline demand. People look at the total number of SDA-eligible participants across Australia or even across a state and assume it means the opportunity is everywhere. It doesn't.

National or state-level figures are useful for context, but they don't help you make good local decisions. Demand in SDA is specific. It varies by postcode, design category, dwelling type, and how many participants are already living in the area. Without that detail, you're just guessing.

Real demand shows up when you drill into the NDIA's data. You need to know how many participants in a particular SA3 or SA4 region are funded for SDA, actively seeking housing, and approved for a specific design category. You also need to compare that to what has already been built or is in the pipeline. That's the level of detail that matters.

Data specialists such as PPC Urban can take the analysis further by drilling down to the SA2 level (typically two to three suburbs, depending on population density). At this scale, they can estimate the current number of SDA participants and model the likely growth of additional participants within an SA2 or across a broader SA3 over the next decade. These assessments are grounded in NDIA data but enhanced through demographic modelling and local planning intelligence to provide investors and providers with a clearer picture of future demand.

There are some other examples. National data might show hundreds of participants needing High Physical Support housing, but when you break it down by region, you might find that in one metro area, there's already a strong pipeline of HPS apartments being delivered, while another region has almost nothing underway. The headline number doesn't tell you that.

In other cases, supply may look strong on paper, causing investors to turn away. Yet SDA data can reveal that local SDA participants are dissatisfied with the quality or suitability of existing SDA dwellings and remain in urgent need of appropriate housing.

This is where oversupply happens. If you rely on broad statistics without checking local demand and pipeline data, you can end up building into a saturated segment. That's when properties sit vacant and investors start to question whether SDA works.

Another issue is relying too heavily on provider opinions. Some investors make decisions based on what one provider says they need. While that might give useful insight, it can also mislead. Providers only see what's in front of them. Their perspective is shaped by their current clients and the properties they manage. It's not the full picture.

Participants are also not as mobile as some people assume. They tend to want to stay in the communities they know. You can't look at demand in one LGA and expect people to move from two hours away to fill your dwelling. It doesn't work like that.

The only way to understand real demand is to go beyond the surface. Headline numbers give you the size of the system. They don't give you location-specific gaps. That's what matters most when you're deciding whether a project makes sense.

Ignore the headlines. Use the data. And always zoom in, seeking guidance from data specialists (such as PPC Urban) for deeper insights.

Using Data Effectively in Investment Decisions

SDA investment only works when it's informed by the right data. That doesn't mean gathering everything available and hoping the picture becomes clear; it means knowing which data points matter, how to read them properly, and how to apply them to a specific site or project.

The most important dataset is the NDIA's SDA demand stack. This includes participants who are already living in SDA, those who are funded and actively seeking housing, and those who are approved but still waiting for funding. Each layer gives a different signal. If you don't understand the difference between them, you risk overestimating real demand.

Next is the pipeline and supply data. You need to know what's already enrolled, what's under construction, and what legacy stock is being retired. This is critical. Many investors forget to subtract the pipeline from their demand figures. They assume the gap is larger than it is, and by the time their project finishes, they're entering a crowded market.

Design category and dwelling type also play a major role. It's not enough to say there's demand for SDA in general. You need to know if it's Improved for Liveability, Fully Accessible, High Physical Support, or Robust. And you need to know whether apartments, villas, or houses are preferred in that specific area. A mismatch here is one of the most common causes of long-term vacancy.

Other factors that affect feasibility include SDA Pricing Arrangements, which set the maximum rent by design type and location. Planning frameworks can also influence timelines and approvals. In Victoria, for example, Clause 52.22 can fast-track certain SDA developments, which has a big impact on project risk. Local authorities may implement the exemption requirements differently depending on their internal policies, interpretation of the planning scheme, and past decisions. Finance constraints matter too. Some postcodes have restrictions on SDA lending. If you don't check that early, you may not be able to secure funding.

Recognising these challenges, PPC Urban has embedded this intelligence into its Data Hub (https://ppcurban.com.au/data-hub/). The platform highlights locations with fewer development restrictions, eligibility for fast-track approvals, and higher lender confidence. Equally, it flags areas where investors should tread cautiously due to financial or regulatory barriers.

The mistakes I see most often include treating expressions of interest or informal enquiries as real demand. They're not. Building based on EOI numbers alone is risky and often leads to oversupply. Another mistake is ignoring category mix. I've seen investors plan for Fully Accessible homes in areas where the unmet need is for Robust or HPS. Without understanding that difference, even a well-built project can fail commercially.

NDIS data is complex, and even experienced SDA investors can struggle with the terminology and datasets. This can lead to confusion or incorrect use of the data, which is why some aggregated "where to invest" strategies may not present the full picture.

I've also seen people fall for marketing that promises guaranteed rental returns without showing how those claims are backed by data. If it sounds too simple, it probably is.

Strong SDA investment decisions are built on layered evidence. Start with the data, test it against the real world, and only move forward if the pieces line up. That's how you avoid chasing hype and start delivering housing that works.

It's also worthwhile mentioning that robust data interpretation doesn't just guide site selection; it also helps investors evaluate and mitigate key risks, including leasing timeframes, vacancy exposure, and achievable rental incomes. In doing so, it turns uncertainty into informed strategy–transforming risk into value.

Demand vs Supply

Understanding demand is only half the equation. The other half is knowing what's already in the pipeline and how it compares to what participants need. This is where many projects go off track. They identify real demand but fail to check whether it's already being met by existing or soon-to-be-completed supply.

Oversupply doesn't always mean thousands of dwellings. In some regions, even a handful of new projects can tip the balance. That's especially true in markets where demand is specific to one design category or dwelling type. If there are already several HPS apartments under construction in the same catchment, building more may not make sense, even if the raw data shows a general shortage of SDA housing.

We've seen examples where participants were funded, had preferences clearly stated, and still didn't move into newly built dwellings. When we looked closer, it wasn't because the properties weren't compliant; it was because they were in the wrong location, didn't match participant needs, or arrived too late in a now-competitive market.

This is proven by the NDIS, which, in its SDA Report (May 2025), states that:

'The NDIA is working to improve SDA housing data. This includes making changes to systems to improve how SDA data is collected and shared. Future system changes will impact data throughout 2025 and 2026, and SDA data will continue to evolve. Changes also aim to support the release of additional information to the market such as more granular location data, SDA vacancy data and data on SDA demand.'

The key is to layer data. Start with NDIA reports to identify where demand exists, then review enrolment data and project pipelines to see what's already being delivered. This includes checking whether dwellings are being tenanted or whether they sat vacant for months after completion. Local provider input can help, but it must be grounded in real figures.

It's important to evaluate the quality and quantity of the existing supply. Sometimes the existing supply looks strong on paper, causing investors to turn away. Yet SDA data can reveal that local SDA participants are dissatisfied with the quality or suitability of existing SDA dwellings and remain in urgent need of appropriate housing.

It's also critical to factor in time. Just because demand exists today doesn't mean it will still be unmet in 12 to 24 months. If your project takes 18 months to deliver and several others are already ahead of you in planning or construction, you may arrive late to a crowded market. SDA is a slow-moving sector, but it's still possible to get caught out if you don't look far enough ahead.

Data experts with deep sector knowledge can forecast the future growth of SDA participants within a given SA3 or SA4, or as small as an SA2 area (comprising two to three suburbs). This forward-looking analysis helps investors identify potential oversupply risks before committing capital. When coupled with an assessment of existing and pipeline housing capacity, it provides a clearer picture of market balance and long-term feasibility.

Some regions are showing signs of saturation. This doesn't always show up in national datasets. You'll see it through persistently high vacancy rates, providers offering incentives to fill rooms, and growing competition to secure referrals. In these areas, caution is essential.

Balancing demand and supply isn't about finding perfect alignment; it's about understanding where risk lies and making decisions based on evidence rather than assumptions. If the pipeline is thin and the data supports unmet need, there's a real opportunity. If the data shows multiple projects already coming online, it may be time to look elsewhere.

SDA investment isn't just about building well; it's about building where it makes sense meeting the needs. That starts with checking your numbers and not just the ones that tell you what you want to hear.

De-Risking with Feasibility Modelling

Once you've validated demand and confirmed there isn't an oversupply risk, the next step is to test the numbers. This is where feasibility modelling comes in. It's the process of translating participants' needs into financial performance. Without it, you're making decisions based on assumptions, not outcomes.

Good feasibility modelling doesn't start with a spreadsheet; it starts with verified data and a clear understanding of unmet service needs or asset types. You need to understand the likely rent based on SDA Pricing Arrangements, participant category mix, and the location of the site. You also need to factor in vacancy assumptions, lease-up timelines, and any density or location rules that could impact approval. A comprehensive, data-driven market assessment ties all these elements together, providing the evidence needed to test feasibility and make confident investment decisions.

A common mistake is assuming full occupancy from day one. That's not how SDA works. Most participants move in gradually. Referrals take time. Even once a provider is engaged, matching participants to the right dwelling can take months. If your model assumes instant income, you're already exposed.

We run sensitivity tests across every scenario. What happens if lease-up takes twice as long? What if one dwelling remains vacant for 12 months? What if build costs increase by 10 percent? The goal is to understand where the pressure points are and whether the project can still work under stress.

Another issue we often see is unrealistic pricing expectations. Just because the SDA Price Guide allows for a certain maximum rent doesn't mean you'll achieve it. Rent levels are influenced by location, participant preferences, and competition. If similar dwellings in the same area are offering lower rates or better amenities, you may have to adjust your forecasts.

We also test against compliance rules. Can the site meet the NDIA's density requirements? Are there zoning restrictions that could delay or block approval? Are there limitations in the planning framework that affect layout or dwelling count? These constraints all feed into the feasibility, even if they don't show up in early-stage calculations.

Feasibility isn't just about confirming whether a project looks profitable; it's a tool for identifying weak spots before you commit capital. If the model only works under perfect conditions, that's a warning sign. A solid SDA project should be able to absorb delays, cost overruns, or slower lease-up without collapsing.

Too many investors treat feasibility as a one-off task. It should be a working document, tested and updated as new information becomes available. The goal isn't to build a perfect model; it's to build a resilient one.

If your numbers only hold up in a best-case scenario, the project probably isn't ready.

When SDA use fails, a specifically designed and built SDA dwelling can revert to the private selling and rental market. If that happens, the returns are usually far lower than expected.

In the private rental market, capital cities typically range from 2.5% to 4.5% gross yield (lower in high-value suburbs like inner Melbourne or Sydney, higher in outer or regional areas). Regional areas can push yields higher, often 4% to 6%, reflecting lower property prices compared to rental demand. By contrast, if an SDA dwelling reverts to the private rental market, the yield could drop to as little as 1%. On resale, property valuations won't account for the higher costs of SDA construction, instead aligning with the value of a standard residential home.

An alternative pathway may be to rent or sell the dwelling to people in need, such as older Australians or those with impairments. The critical question for investors is: 'Have you assessed the market size of these potential occupants and developed a clear exit strategy?'

The Road Ahead for SDA Data and Policy

Over the next 5 to 10 years, demand for SDA will continue to grow. We expect to see a consistent need for High Physical Support and Robust housing, particularly as more legacy dwellings are phased out and more participants undergo housing assessments. That part of the trend is steady and predictable.

We'll also see demand expand beyond capital cities. Regional hubs are starting to show clearer data on SDA-eligible participants, and as support services improve in those areas, more people will choose to stay in their local communities. This shift will create new opportunities, but only for those who are paying attention to the local signals.

What we need now is better and more frequent data at the local level. NDIA reporting has improved, but gaps remain. We need more transparency around upcoming supply, more clarity around how demand is defined, and better alignment between datasets. This will help providers and investors make informed decisions based on what's happening, not just what's assumed.

We also need more consistency in planning frameworks. Right now, every council and state has its own interpretation of what SDA looks like from a land use and zoning perspective. This creates delays, confusion, and unnecessary cost. A more unified approach would reduce risk and support faster delivery of compliant dwellings in the right locations.

Finally, we need stronger oversight of marketing practices in this space. Too many investors are being sold the idea of guaranteed occupancy or inflated rental returns without any supporting evidence. These claims distort the market and increase the risk of oversupply in areas that can't sustain it. Clearer expectations and more accountability would protect everyone involved, especially participants.

The answer isn't complicated. Investors, lenders, and the NDIA all need to better understand the value of using independent advice from data experts who specialise in the NDIS sector. Avoid advice from those with conflicts of interest: builders, developers, or doggy providers tied to sales. Independent, evidence-based guidance shows the real risks and opportunities.

If there's one message I'd leave with providers and investors, it's this—don't build to the headline. Invest with evidence, guided by independent advice.

From Data to Impact

SDA is often presented as a once-in-a-generation opportunity, and in some ways, it is. It offers a rare chance to deliver real housing outcomes for people with disability while also creating long-term, stable investment returns. But that opportunity only exists when projects are backed by the right thinking. And the right thinking starts with data.

There's a difference between having access to information and knowing how to use it. The data is already out there: NDIA reports, demand stacks, pipeline dashboards, pricing guides, planning maps, it's all available. What's missing in most cases is the discipline to analyse it properly and the judgment to apply it in the right way.

The best SDA projects I've seen didn't happen by accident. They were deliberate. They were built on a clear understanding of who the housing was for, what type of dwelling was most suitable, and whether the area had the support infrastructure to sustain it. They weren't chasing volume or vague ideas of demand; they were built for purpose, based on evidence.

This is what separates successful SDA investments from those that struggle. The successful ones take a structured approach. They validate demand, assess supply, model risk conservatively, and track policy changes closely. They don't overbuild. They don't rely on assumptions. They certainly don't take advice from a single source.

There will always be people in the market who promise shortcuts, guaranteed leases, high yields, and no-risk opportunities. But SDA is not a shortcut; it's a specialised market that requires careful planning, technical knowledge, and long-term commitment. When it's done well, the results speak for themselves: stable income, low vacancies, and real impact on people's lives. The challenge isn't to be first; it's to be accurate. This isn't about racing to build the most dwellings or fill a portfolio as quickly as possible; it's about making smart, evidence-based decisions that hold up over time.

At PPC Urban, our goal is to help providers and investors see clearly. That means cutting through sales pitches, translating raw data into insight, and supporting projects that serve the people they're meant to. And in 2025, we launched PPC Urban's Data Hub – a real-time, nationwide location-intelligence platform for childcare and disability housing, with more sectors on the way. It gives you instant visibility of demand, supply, demographics and planning constraints, so you can make faster, evidence-based decisions with confidence. If you'd like a trusted partner on your investment journey, reach out anytime. We can show you a quick demo and how our clients use it to reduce risk and speed up feasibility.

Good SDA projects don't just meet compliance. They meet demand. The data already knows the difference. The question is, are you using it?

CHAPTER 8

UNLOCKING SUPPLY THROUGH SMARTER INVESTMENT—WHERE TO FROM HERE

BY BRAD FULLER

○

Brad Fuller is a leader in Specialist Disability Accommodation (SDA) and a passionate advocate for inclusive, participant-centred housing. As the founding director and CEO of Brighter Living Australia, Brad leads a team committed to helping people with disability find homes where every ability can shine, and where lived experience is valued through inclusive employment. His ability to connect property expertise with authentic advocacy for people with disability has made him a trusted voice in the SDA space.

Prior to founding Brighter Living Australia, Brad co-founded Everhomes Group, a Queensland-based SDA provider, which he grew, alongside his daughter and son-in-law, into one of the sector's standout success stories, managing over 150 homes within three years.

• • •

CONNECT WITH BRAD AT:
WEBSITE: brighterliving.com.au
LINKED IN: @brad-fuller-97624b328

Introduction—Where to From Here

When SDA first entered the NDIS landscape, there was genuine excitement. It represented a new opportunity, not just for investment, but for improving housing outcomes for people with disability. The concept was straightforward: build homes that are fit for purpose, offer better quality of life for participants, and create a viable investment pathway for those wanting to support social infrastructure.

In those early years, many developers and investors moved quickly. Some were driven by ethics, others by returns, and often by a mix of both. But without consistent guidelines or clear data, decisions were made based on assumptions. Properties were built in areas where land was affordable, but access to essential services was limited. Some homes met compliance standards but failed to meet participant expectations.

Today, the landscape looks very different. Funding has tightened. Vacancy rates have increased in some regions. We're seeing properties that can't attract tenants, while in other areas, participants still struggle to find suitable accommodation. The result is a market that feels out of balance. Oversupply exists in pockets, but so does unmet demand. And providers are left navigating uncertainty.

This chapter is not a sales pitch for SDA, and it's not a warning to avoid it either. My goal is to provide a clear-eyed view of where things stand, how we got here, and what providers need to consider if they want to be part of SDA's future. I've worked with a wide range of providers, developers, investors, and participants, and I've seen the sector from multiple angles. SDA still holds value, but it requires a smarter and more participant-led approach.

In the sections that follow, I'll walk through:

- The early drivers of SDA investment and why they created some of the current challenges
- What's happening with supply, demand, and funding in the market today
- Why some homes succeed while others sit empty
- What providers can do now to make more informed and ethical decisions about SDA

If you're thinking about offering SDA, or you're already in the space and wondering how to navigate the current pressures, this chapter is for you. The aim isn't to complicate the conversation but to help bring some clarity to what has become a complex area of the NDIS.

It's essential to understand what has changed and how to respond to it. SDA can still work, but only if we shift the focus back to where it should have been all along—on the people who are going to live in these homes.

The Rise of SDA Investment

When SDA was introduced into the NDIS, it got a lot of attention. For many, it looked like a chance to do something positive while building a long-term income stream. The returns were strong, payments were funded by the government, and at first, there were very few limits on where and how you could get involved.

In those early years, people entered the market from all angles. Some were genuinely focused on participants and outcomes. Others saw an opportunity and followed the money. The message at the time was simple: SDA is funded, and there is demand, so build and they will come.

The problem was, there weren't any clear guidelines to start with, and the data just wasn't there. A lot of providers and developers made decisions based on land price, not participant demand. It made financial sense on paper, but it didn't match what people needed in real life.

Western Melbourne is a good example. Developers were building homes in Wyndham Vale and other areas because the land was cheap. But participants in those areas often didn't have access to the services they rely on: hospitals, Allied Health, and transport. So even though the homes were technically compliant, they weren't practical for the people they were meant to support.

Another issue was design. A lot of the early homes ticked the minimum boxes for SDA, but they didn't offer anything beyond that. Small rooms, no outdoor space, low-quality finishes—they weren't homes that stood out to participants. And since participants don't pay rent directly, they have the choice to go where something better is on offer. That part of the equation was missed by many early developers.

At the same time, the market was booming. Builders were busy, funders were interested, and homes were going up fast. But because there was no density control, we started to see oversupply in certain regions. Some builders were completing properties that had no participants lined up and no support services nearby. Now, those properties are sitting vacant.

That's when things began to shift. The banks became more cautious. Funders started blacklisting certain postcodes. If you're in an oversupplied region now, it can be hard to get funding or sell a finished property. Builders are reporting zero sales in those areas. The demand hasn't disappeared, but the homes are in the wrong places.

This has created serious pressure for providers and investors who got in early without fully understanding how participant choice and infrastructure access drive tenancy. It's been a hard learning curve, but it's also a natural part of a new market maturing.

Despite all this, I still believe SDA is a good opportunity. But it's no longer about fast returns or broad assumptions. It's about building the right home in the right place, for the right person. That means understanding local demand, working closely with stakeholders, and taking the time to design something people want to live in.

The early wave of investment built the foundation. What we do next will decide whether the sector grows in a sustainable way or stays stuck in a cycle of poor planning and underutilised housing.

What Went Wrong

A lot of people entered the SDA space with the right intentions, but without clear guidelines, accurate data, or a proper understanding of how participant demand works, some critical mistakes were made.

One of the main problems was the data. The information used to decide where and what to build hasn't always reflected what's happening on the ground. Much of the data is at least three months behind, and even when it's current, it doesn't show whether homes are funded or if they've ever had participants living in them.

We also have legacy homes in the system. These are older government-built properties that still show up in the SDA data as available. These homes often don't meet current design standards, and many haven't been upgraded, but because they're technically listed, they distort the picture.

So when a provider looks at the demand in a region, it can seem like there's already a lot of housing available, when the homes aren't suitable or haven't been used. This leads to a mismatch. On paper, some areas look oversupplied, but many of the properties in those areas don't meet participant expectations. At the same time, areas with real demand may not have any viable options at all. This creates problems for both providers and participants.

Funding has also become harder to access. Many lenders are more cautious now. Some have stopped funding SDA in certain suburbs altogether. These decisions are based on what they're seeing in the market. Homes have been built in areas with no basic infrastructure, no transport, no services, and no demand. Even if the build is high quality, it doesn't work if the location isn't right.

This is where many early projects fell short. SDA isn't just about building something that meets minimum design standards; it has to fit into a person's life. A house that's compliant but far from a hospital, therapy providers, or family support isn't going to be a first choice. Participants will always choose the home that gives them the best quality of life, not just the one that's available.

A lot of early investment also came off the back of advice that was over-simplified. People were told SDA was a guaranteed return because it was government-funded, but that left out a key part of the equation. Participants choose where they live. If the home doesn't meet their needs, they won't move in.

This has created real issues. Homes are sitting vacant, not because there's no demand, but because the properties were built in the wrong locations. In some cases, there's no Supported Independent Living provider nearby. In others, there's no access to services or transport. These are basics that were overlooked.

Some builders now have entire streets of completed homes with no sales. Some providers have houses that have never had a single tenancy. This isn't always a reflection of poor construction; it's often a sign that the early planning didn't take participant needs into account.

Yet, there are still more than 15,000 participants who have SDA funding and aren't living in a suitable home. That tells us the demand is still there. But those people are waiting for homes that work for them. They're not going to settle for a box that ticks a compliance list if it doesn't support their lifestyle.

This situation has put pressure on everyone. Investors are holding properties that aren't performing. Participants are frustrated by the lack of real choice. Families and support teams are left trying to find workarounds when a proper solution should already exist.

These are real problems affecting real people, which is why things have to change. Providers can't rely on broad averages or generic data anymore. Decisions need to be based on local knowledge, service access, and participant demand.

The providers who are getting it right now are the ones who have built strong local relationships. They're working with participants, families, hospitals, support coordinators, and SILs. They understand that SDA sits within a broader support system. It doesn't operate in isolation.

Where the sector goes from here depends on whether we learn from these mistakes. There's still time to do that, but it starts with being honest about what hasn't worked and committing to doing things differently going forward.

Designing for People, Not Portfolios

One of the most common mistakes I see is providers treating SDA like a property investment portfolio, rather than a housing and support solution for real people. The focus shifts to yield, depreciation, and how many houses can be delivered, rather than whether anyone wants to live in them.

Participants don't choose properties based on your cost per square metre; they choose based on how the home feels, how it works for their needs, and how connected it is to the life they want to live.

A lot of homes have been designed to meet minimum requirements, but that's not enough anymore. The SDA Design Standard is the starting point, not the goal. Compliance alone doesn't make a property attractive. It might be legally eligible, but if it has tiny rooms, no outdoor area, poor ventilation, or bad natural light, people are going to look elsewhere.

Participants have options now. They're comparing homes. If you're offering a narrow hallway, basic finishes, and a backyard the size of a car park, and someone else has a home with space, light, tech-enabled features, and access to services, the decision is obvious.

It's not just about features; it's about how those features support independence and dignity. Automation, for example, makes a real difference. Things like voice-controlled lighting, blinds, or entry systems aren't luxuries; they're tools that support daily living and reduce reliance on staff.

The location is just as important. I often say that a good SDA home is within 30 kilometres of a major CBD or regional centre. That gives you a better chance of meeting participant needs in terms of hospitals, community services, transport, and lifestyle options. It also makes the property more viable in the long run.

You have to think beyond the four walls. If a participant can't access their GP, their day program, their friends, or their family, they are going to feel isolated. It doesn't matter how good the kitchen is if the person can't get to their physio appointment. These are the things that drive tenancy decisions.

I've seen firsthand the impact a well-designed, well-located home can have. One participant moved from an older group home into a new purpose-built SDA home. Within weeks, there was a noticeable shift. Their mood changed, their confidence improved, and they were engaging more in daily life. They felt safe, comfortable, and respected. That environment gave them the space to grow. That's the outcome we should be aiming for.

But to get there, providers need to ask better questions at the planning stage. Who is the home for? What supports are nearby? Is there access to public transport? Can a participant get to the local shops, their church, or their support team? Is the street safe and quiet? Would you live there?

A home isn't just a set of physical specifications; it's a living environment. And it has to be developed with the participant's quality of life in mind.

I also encourage providers to involve support coordinators, participants, and families in the planning stage. Ask them what works and what doesn't. Build homes based on real-world experience, not just architectural drawings. You'll learn more from a 15-minute chat with a support coordinator than from a three-hour spreadsheet.

The providers who are successful in this space aren't the ones building the most houses; they're the ones building the right houses in the right places, with the right people around the table.

There's still an opportunity to lift the standard of SDA in this country, but that means shifting away from a compliance mindset and towards a participant-led design approach. It's not about ticking boxes; it's about building homes people want to live in.

Building for the Future

SDA still has a place in the market, but the way we approach it needs to change. It's not new anymore. We're in a different environment now. The rules, the funding, the risks, they've all shifted.

A lot of people got into SDA thinking it was a simple model: build a compliant home, and participants will come. That worked for a while. But the market has moved on. Now, providers need to slow down and plan properly. You can't just build where the land is cheap and expect it to fill.

If there's no infrastructure around the home, participants won't choose it. That includes hospitals, public transport, day programs, shops, and support services. If those things aren't nearby, the house might sit vacant. It doesn't matter how well it's built if no one wants to live there.

Start with the participant. Think about who the home is for and what they need access to. Is the home close to family? Can they get to their GP or therapy? Is there a support coordinator or SIL provider nearby? These are basic questions, but too many providers skip them.

Location matters. Most participants want to be within 30 kilometres of a major centre. That gives them better access to services and connection to community. If you're building in fringe suburbs or regional pockets with no infrastructure, it's going to be hard to fill that home.

It's not just about geography; it's about design too. You can't just meet the minimum design standards and think that's enough. Participants compare homes. If one house has small bedrooms, no automation, and no outdoor space, and the next has open layouts, good lighting, and proper smart tech, that's an easy decision.

And design isn't about luxury; it's about function. Automation can reduce reliance on staff and increase independence. A larger yard can mean more outdoor time. A well-located home makes it easier for participants to engage in their community.

The funding environment has also changed. Lenders are much more cautious now. They want to see strong financials. In some cases, they won't even look at a project unless you can show service infrastructure in the area and a clear path to tenancy.

If you're building SDA, you need to understand your numbers. How much will the build cost? How long can you carry the loan if the house sits vacant? What's your fallback plan? These aren't small details; they're the difference between a sustainable business and one that collapses under pressure.

It's also about your process. If you're just trying to push houses into the market, people will pick up on that. Families talk. Support coordinators talk. If your property is all compliance and no connection to real needs, they'll move on.

The providers who are getting it right now are the ones who build relationships. They're not just dropping flyers in inboxes; they're talking to support coordinators, connecting with hospitals, walking through the local area to understand how participants actually live.

They're visible. They take feedback before the home is finished. They adjust designs to suit what participants have asked for. That sort of engagement builds trust. It also leads to better outcomes.

I don't think we have too many SDA homes overall. I think we have too many in the wrong places, built without the right planning. The next wave of SDA needs to be more deliberate. Fewer homes that are better located, properly designed, and backed by providers who understand the responsibility that comes with it.

If you're entering the sector now or trying to grow, it's not about volume; it's about quality and fit. The homes need to work, not just for the participant, but for the provider, the support team, and the wider system around them.

This is a long-term space. It's not about fast wins. The providers who stay focused on participants and build with care will still do well.

What Providers Must Do Now

If you're looking at SDA today, you need to approach it differently. What worked five years ago doesn't always hold now. The environment has shifted, and providers need to shift with it.

Start with a clear understanding of who the home is for. Too many projects are still being planned around land prices or construction timelines without any real clarity on the participant. If you don't know who you're designing for, it's very hard to get the location, layout, or partnerships right.

Location is a major factor. Not just where land is available, but where someone would choose to live. That means access to transport, to hospitals, to services like Allied Health and SIL. It also means being near family, friends, and local communities. A house might be new and fully compliant, but if it's isolated or disconnected from services, participants will look elsewhere.

Talk to the people who already understand the area. Support coordinators and SIL providers have a much clearer picture of where the demand is and what's working. They can also tell you what is being avoided and why. That kind of insight is more useful than any market report.

It's important to talk to them early. Before you build. Before you commit to the block. Once the house is finished, there's not much you can do if the location is wrong.

You also need to be realistic about your own capacity. Can your business carry a property that sits empty for six months? Maybe longer? Because that's happening now. It's no longer a safe assumption that a property will fill straight away. You need to factor in risk and timeframes and make sure you can sustain that.

Your internal systems also need to be tight. Who's responsible for compliance? Who handles funding claims? Who manages relationships with participants and families? This can't be an afterthought. If the back end is disorganised, it shows. Participants and stakeholders can see it, and it affects how your service is perceived.

When it comes to promoting the property, be honest. Don't oversell or exaggerate features. Describe the home accurately. Show photos that match what people will see in real life. Support coordinators are reviewing multiple options, and they talk to each other. Your reputation matters, especially if you're planning to grow.

One of the simplest things you can do is open the house to people early. Bring in local stakeholders for a walkthrough. Let them give feedback. You'll get more value from one on-site conversation than from a dozen marketing emails. It also shows you're listening and willing to adjust.

The providers who are staying steady right now are the ones who keep things simple. They stay close to their network. They take the time to ask questions. They follow up. They don't assume demand, they confirm it.

SDA doesn't work in isolation; it depends on the quality of the design, the location, the provider, and the relationships around it. If even one of those pieces is missing, it's hard to get a good outcome.

You don't need to overcomplicate it, but you do need to be thoughtful, practical, and consistent. If you're building homes that are informed by participant needs, supported by your network, and backed by solid planning, then you're heading in the right direction.

Final Word—Where to From Here

The SDA space has changed. What used to be a high-growth, loosely structured environment is becoming more defined. The early wave of activity has given way to a more cautious, more informed phase. That's not a bad thing; it means the sector is maturing.

But that shift also brings new expectations. Participants and families are asking better questions. Stakeholders are comparing homes more closely. Funders are taking a harder look at location, design, and financial sustainability. Everyone is more aware of what can go wrong when SDA is rushed or poorly planned.

This is the point where providers need to decide what role they want to play. If you're just looking to build a few houses and move on, this is probably not the right time to enter the market. The risk is too high. But if you're serious about doing SDA properly, and you're willing to take the time to understand the environment, there's still a strong case to be part of it.

I still believe in the value of the model. When SDA is done right, the impact is clear. Participants move into a home that works for them. Their independence increases. Their health improves. Support costs often go down. Families report reduced stress. Service providers can deliver better outcomes with less complexity.

Getting to that outcome takes more than a compliant design and a good-looking brochure; it takes a clear understanding of what makes a location viable. It takes early engagement with support coordinators and health professionals. It takes patience when filling homes and discipline when managing funding and compliance.

It also takes the right mindset. SDA isn't passive income; it requires active involvement, continuous learning, and long-term thinking. It's a part of the NDIS that's still evolving, and providers need to evolve with it.

The question to ask isn't just 'Can I build this home?' It's 'Will someone want to live in it?' If the answer is no, go back and rethink it. That's where a lot of providers went wrong the first time. The home was treated as a product, not a place to live.

We're at a point now where the sector can correct that. There are still opportunities, but they come with responsibility. If you're going to be in SDA, it has to be for the right reasons. It has to be based on participant needs, and it has to deliver long-term value, not just financial return.

If you've built homes that aren't performing, it's worth revisiting them. Can you reconfigure the design? Can you engage new partners or bring in specialist tenancy support? Vacancy doesn't always mean failure. Sometimes it means you need to reconnect with the people the home was meant for.

If you're just getting started, slow down. Take the time to understand what works in this sector. Talk to the people who've done it before. Look at where others have gone wrong and learn from that. The information is available now. The stories are there. You don't need to repeat the same mistakes.

There's still a place in this market for providers who are thoughtful, transparent, and committed to doing it properly. SDA isn't broken; it just needs better planning and stronger alignment with the people it's meant to serve.

If the outcome works for the participant, the model can work, but it has to start there. Every time.

CHAPTER 9

RETHINKING THE SDA ECOSYSTEM

BY DEBBIE KINDNESS

○

Debbie Kindness is general manager of NDIS Property Australia, bringing over two decades of experience in tourism, finance, and property. Since joining the company in mid-2020, she's been instrumental in its growth from a two-person operation to a 20+ member team. Debbie's leadership has been pivotal in marketing and selling NDIS investment properties, coordinating with builders, designers, lenders, and providers to ensure the successful development of SDA properties across Australia.

• • •

CONNECT WITH DEBBIE AT:
WEBSITE: ndis.property
LINKED IN: @debbie-kindness-930a2123b

SDA is an Ecosystem

Specialist Disability Accommodation (SDA) isn't just about bricks, mortar, and floor plans. It works best when we see it as an ecosystem—a living network of people, services, and opportunities. Homes only truly come to life when everyone involved—developers, investors, providers, participants, families, and government—work together. When that collaboration is missing, even the most impressive-looking property can fall short of its main purpose: supporting people to live with dignity, independence, and real community connection.

It's tempting to think of SDA like any other property investment—build it and the right tenant will turn up. But SDA is different. It's not about simply putting a roof over someone's head. These are homes designed for people with significant support needs, where the measure of success isn't square footage or finishes, but whether someone can actually live well there.

That's why the 'right match' is so important. An SDA home must work with a person's support needs, lifestyle preferences, and NDIS funding. A design that looks perfect in an architect's drawings may not be practical in daily life. A suburb that looks great on a spreadsheet may leave someone far from family, friends, or essential services. SDA is not about ticking boxes; it's about building the right partnerships so people can choose a home that truly fits.

At the centre of all this are the participants. Each has their own goals, preferences, and rights. If we only chase financial returns, we lose sight of what makes SDA life-changing. Long-term success comes from understanding the people we're building for, taking a future-focused view, and building trust.

Developers and investors play a critical role in creating the foundations, but the real value emerges when the right voices are included early on: support coordinators, therapists, SIL providers, and most importantly, the participants themselves and their families. That's when we see homes that are both strong investments and genuinely ready for life from the very first day.

SDA isn't just about building for people; it's about building *with* people. That's when the ecosystem thrives.

Where the System is Breaking Down

The NDIS was built on strong foundations–choice and control. But as with any large system, the reality can sometimes fall short of the vision. One area where we still see challenges is in how Specialist Disability Accommodation (SDA) and Supported Independent Living (SIL) fit together. While the two are funded separately, they need to operate side by side if we want homes that aren't just accessible, but truly liveable and sustainable.

Some of the roadblocks come from the way policies play out in practice. Take the common 1:3 support ratio, for example. It's efficient on paper, but it doesn't always reflect what participants want. Many people prefer smaller, more personalised living arrangements, yet the funding model often pushes developments toward larger group homes. This has created a gap between what's being built and what participants want.

Location can also be a sticking point. Much of the current SDA development has been driven by land prices or investment returns, rather than participant needs. This has led to homes being built in areas far from family, friends, transport, or services. On paper, these homes meet every compliance requirement, but in reality, they can leave residents feeling isolated, and that's not what SDA was designed to achieve.

Another common challenge comes up at the matching stage. Too often, participants are brought in after the home has already been built. By then, it's too late to make meaningful adjustments. The result? Homes that don't quite fit, costly modifications, or, in the worst cases, properties sitting empty. This doesn't just waste money, it undermines participant choice and control, leaving people feeling like they have to take what's available rather than what truly suits their lives.

Behind the scenes, there's also a problem with information sharing. Developers may not know what the actual housing demand is in a particular area, while SIL providers may not have visibility of what's coming down the pipeline. Without a shared pool of accurate data, it's hard to plan effectively.

We also see that participants can struggle to qualify for SDA when eligibility criteria are applied too rigidly; even people with very high support needs can miss out on housing that would completely change their lives.

These challenges aren't isolated; they're interconnected. And they won't be solved by any one group working alone. What's needed is more collaboration, better transparency, and earlier involvement of participants in the process. If we can line up housing, supports, and personal goals from the start, the system can deliver on its original promise—real choice and real control for the people it's meant to serve.

The Role of Ethical Investment

For SDA to truly achieve its purpose, investment has to do more than generate a return. It needs to deliver both financial security and meaningful outcomes for people with disability. This isn't about charity; it's about recognising that the most sustainable investments are the ones built around genuine demand, thoughtful design, and long-term value.

Of course, the financial side matters. SDA projects require significant capital, careful planning, and an understanding of complex regulations. But the strongest financial results come when homes are designed and located in ways that people actually want to live in. A property that's poorly designed or built in the wrong spot may look like a sound investment on paper, but it will struggle to attract and retain tenants. In SDA, doing good and doing well are two sides of the same coin.

That's why we encourage investors to widen their lens. Instead of focusing only on yields, ask questions like: Who will this home suit? How will it support daily life? Will it still work five or ten years from now? These questions lead to better design choices, smarter locations, and stronger partnerships with providers.

The most future-proof strategies embrace co-design. By listening to participants, families, and SIL providers from the start, we can prioritise features that really matter, whether that's durable finishes, technology that supports independence, flexible layouts, or outdoor spaces that promote calm and connection. Yes, these choices may add slightly to the upfront cost, but they pay back through satisfied tenants, long-term leases, and a trusted reputation in the market.

Treating SDA as a quick property play is risky. Homes rushed to market without careful thought might fill temporarily, but as more supply comes online, participants will have greater choice. Over time, quality will always win.

SDA is strongest when investors see themselves as long-term partners in creating homes that truly change lives. Those who understand the dual purpose—financial sustainability and social impact—will not only achieve stable returns but will also leave a lasting legacy of housing that works for people. In this sector, that's the kind of outcome that benefits everyone.

The Case for Collaboration

If there's one lesson SDA keeps teaching us, it's this—housing is never a solo effort. It takes a whole team to get it right. Yet too often, SDA projects play out like a relay race where the baton keeps being dropped. Builders hand over to providers, providers hand over to SIL teams, and participants are only invited in at the very end. The result? Homes that meet the rules but don't always meet real life.

The solution isn't more red tape; it's smarter collaboration. True success comes when the right people are at the table from day one and stay involved all the way through. The foundation of a strong SDA project isn't just the concrete slab; it's the relationships.

Bringing SIL providers into the conversation before designs are finalised can completely change the outcome. Support coordinators can flag whether a location and design works for participants' daily routines. Builders who understand how supports are delivered can make small but critical design adjustments—maybe shifting a wall, adding a breakout space, or including an extra bathroom. These tweaks may seem minor on paper, but they can save enormous costs later and, more importantly, create homes that genuinely work from day one.

This is where the idea of an 'anchor tenant' becomes powerful. An SIL provider who knows their participants' needs can help shape a home that's fit for purpose before it's even built. That gives residents a better living experience and gives investors greater confidence in long-term occupancy.

Collaboration also cuts down on waste. When conversations happen early, we avoid endless redesigns and expensive retrofits. But it requires us to bridge different perspectives. Builders think in square metres, SIL providers think in care models, and investors think in yields. Without a common goal, these priorities can clash. With the right process, they align around the shared purpose of creating homes that people want to live in.

The best projects we see are never perfect, but they're united. When everyone works together, participants get a home that supports their lives, SIL providers get spaces that allow them to deliver quality care, and investors enjoy stable, long-term returns.

In SDA, collaboration isn't just nice to have; it's the difference between a house and a home.

Policy Levers and System Fixes

SDA started with a bold and inspiring idea—to use market innovation to create homes that are safe, accessible, and empowering for people with significant disability. That vision is still strong, but as the sector has grown, some of the policies and processes haven't kept pace with what's happening on the ground. The good news? Most of the fixes we need aren't radical overhauls—they're practical, achievable adjustments.

One of the biggest opportunities is in how we share and use data. Right now, it's surprisingly hard to get a clear local picture of what participants need. The NDIA holds valuable insights about where people live, their funding levels, and eligibility, but this information doesn't reach the providers and developers trying to build solutions. Without it, supply can drift off course—homes are built where there's already plenty, while gaps in other areas remain unfilled. Participants end up with fewer genuine choices simply because the right homes weren't built in the right places.

Design is another area ready for a refresh. The SDA Design Standard, introduced in 2019, was an important milestone, but since then, we've learned so much more about what makes a home *liveable*. Accessibility is the foundation, but it's not the whole story. Natural light, calming spaces, sensory-friendly design, and layouts that support independence all matter just as much. A co-designed update that has been shaped by the voices of residents, families, and support teams is well overdue and would go a long way towards bringing the standard in line with the sector's lived experience and emerging technology.

Funding models could also use more flexibility. The system's preference for a 1:3 support ratio might work for some, but it doesn't fit everyone. Some people thrive in smaller shared settings, others need one-on-one support, and still others prefer innovative models in between. Providers often struggle to balance these personalised approaches with financial sustainability under the current rules. A little more flexibility would go a long way toward matching funding to real life.

Eligibility is another area worth revisiting. At times, the criteria are interpreted so tightly that people with very high needs can miss out on housing that would change their lives. Broadening the approach without losing safeguards could help ensure SDA reaches everyone who can genuinely benefit.

Most importantly, the NDIA and the sector need to work in closer partnership. This isn't about top-down decisions; it's about ongoing dialogue. Sharing insights, running joint pilot programs, and holding inclusive workshops are all practical steps that could strengthen trust and align practice with policy.

These adjustments won't just result in more houses being built; they'll result in more *homes* that people want to live in. That's the true measure of whether SDA is delivering on its promise.

What 'Better' Looks Like

The SDA sector is steadily maturing. We're seeing smarter investors, more thoughtful designs, and a welcome shift away from simply meeting the minimum standards toward creating homes that genuinely help people thrive. And that's exactly what SDA should be about—not just a roof overhead, but a place that supports long-term wellbeing, dignity, and community connection.

One of the biggest shifts has been moving away from the idea of a static 'forever home' and towards flexible, adaptable living. The real question now is: 'Can this home evolve as someone's needs change?' A truly permanent home remains the right choice year after year because it adapts with the resident, not against them.

The best homes we see are designed with this flexibility built in. They might include quiet breakout spaces for sensory regulation, wider doorways to allow for future technology, or second living areas that make life easier for both residents and support staff. These features often add very little to construction costs, but they make a huge difference to a home's comfort, functionality, and longevity.

We're also seeing promising new models emerge. Vertical villages—purpose-built apartment buildings—concentrate SDA supply in one location. They give residents privacy and independence while allowing SIL providers to deliver support more efficiently. Done well, they also create a vibrant, connected community. At the other end of the spectrum, custom pods on family land or in quieter settings offer highly personalised solutions and a deep sense of ownership and belonging. In between, we're seeing options like small clusters of villas or self-contained units within a larger house. These combine the best of both worlds—privacy and autonomy for residents, with the added benefits of a social environment and streamlined support for SIL teams.

This progress is also being powered by more intentional capital. Investors are asking the right questions upfront: 'How will this design affect daily life? What are the risks around tenancy? How can we create a home people will choose to stay in long term?' This mindset shift from chasing short-term returns to building sustainable outcomes is driving higher quality across the board.

Most importantly, the voices of participants are shaping the future more directly than ever. People with lived experience are telling us what works, what doesn't, and what's missing. That feedback is invaluable, and it's holding the entire sector accountable to SDA's original purpose.

The goal isn't to create perfect homes; it's to keep learning, improving, and building better with every project. When we listen to participants, apply evidence, and keep quality at the centre, the sector will continue to move closer to what SDA was always meant to be—housing that truly changes lives.

The Next Five Years

Looking ahead, the next five years will be critical for SDA. The sector has already proven it can deliver high-quality, innovative housing at scale, but the challenge now is to make sure that growth translates into genuine choice and better outcomes for participants.

The first priority is getting supply and demand into closer alignment. Too often, we still see homes sitting empty in some regions while participants elsewhere struggle to find a suitable option. Smarter use of NDIA data, coupled with greater transparency from providers, will help direct investment where it's needed most. When the right homes are built in the right places, everyone wins—participants, providers, and investors alike.

Policy reform will also shape the years ahead. We're likely to see updates to the SDA Design Standard, reflecting the lessons of the past five years and the lived experience of residents. It would also be great to see funding models evolving to allow more flexibility in support ratios and tenancy arrangements. These changes, if co-designed with the sector, could unlock new models of living that better match people's preferences and needs.

Technology will play a growing role too. From smart-home automation that enhances independence, to assistive technologies that lighten the load on support staff, the next wave of innovation will reshape how people live in—and with—their homes. Importantly, this isn't about gadgets for the sake of it; it's about practical tools that make daily life safer, easier, and more empowering.

We'll also see a stronger focus on integration with community. SDA can't exist in isolation. Homes need to be part of vibrant neighbourhoods where people can access work, education, recreation, and social opportunities. Expect to see more emphasis on location and connection, not just compliance with minimum design standards.

If the sector can get these things right—aligning supply and demand, refining policy, embracing technology, and embedding community—SDA will fulfil its promise. It won't just deliver housing; it will deliver *homes* that change lives.

The next five years are not just about building more; they're about building better, together.

Conclusion—Building SDA That Lasts

Specialist Disability Accommodation is more than bricks and mortar; it's a carefully balanced ecosystem—a collaboration between investors, developers, SDA providers, SIL teams, support coordinators, participants, and their families. Each party has a unique role, and when those roles align early and clearly, the results can be transformative.

Success isn't measured simply by compliance or occupancy rates; it's measured by homes that empower participants to live with dignity, independence, and connection. Homes where support is practical, flexible, and personalised. Homes where participants and families feel genuinely heard and included in every stage of planning, design, and delivery.

We've also seen that SDA works best when investment and ethics go hand-in-hand. Investors who consider long-term sustainability, tenant satisfaction, and community integration, along with financial return, help create homes that last, both physically and socially. Designers, builders, and providers who engage early and collaborate openly help prevent costly retrofits and ensure homes are fit for purpose from day one. And policy, when applied thoughtfully, provides the structure and flexibility needed to support innovation and choice.

Looking forward, the next five years are a chance to embed these lessons into every SDA project. Smarter data, more flexible funding, inclusive design, and community-focused development will allow the sector to meet growing demand while improving outcomes for participants. Technology and innovation will continue to enhance independence, and ongoing collaboration will ensure homes remain functional, adaptable, and deeply human.

At its heart, SDA is about people. When the sector centres participants' voices, aligns stakeholders around shared goals, and plans for long-term sustainability, the outcomes ripple out: participants thrive, providers deliver better care, investors achieve stable returns, and communities become more inclusive.

This is the future of SDA—not just housing, but homes that truly change lives. It's within our reach, and it's worth building together.

CHAPTER 10

DEVELOPING QUALITY SDA HOMES

BY ANGAD SINGH

Angad Singh is the co-founder of Develop Capital, helping investors build long-term wealth through property development. By combining the safety of brick-and-mortar assets, the value-add of development, and the strength of inner-city markets, Develop Capital creates reliable, done-for-you returns for savvy investors all around Australia. Through its SDA delivery arm Nirvana Lifestyles, Angad and his team focus on high-quality homes that prioritise both participant outcomes and long-term value.

Outside work, Angad is a husband and proud father to a baby daughter. He enjoys travelling, connecting with entrepreneurs and property developers, and exploring big ideas in business, philosophy, and life!

• • •

CONNECT WITH ANGAD AT:
WEBSITE: developcapital.com.au

From Dentist to Developer

Property wasn't always part of my career plan; I started out as a dentist and ran my own practice for over 10 years. But early on, I took on a small development project. It was just five houses on a block, but that experience changed everything. I realised I enjoyed the process of building and developing homes more than the work I was trained to do.

For a while, I managed both - dentistry during the day, development work on the side. The more I built, the more I wanted to understand how the process all worked. Property is complex. It's creative. It forces you to solve real problems and learn from every decision. I never felt like I was repeating the same day, which was something I appreciated.

Eventually, I understood that to succeed in development, I needed to control the parts of the process where things often go wrong. That's when we started bringing everything under one roof. We created our own construction business, managed projects directly, and built a team that could handle each stage properly. It wasn't about growth for its own sake; it was about doing things well and reducing risk.

Nirvana Lifestyles came out of that work. We set it up to focus specifically on specialist disability accommodation (SDA) because we saw a real need. Too many projects in this space were being led by people who didn't fully understand the purpose of SDA or the experience of the people who would live in these homes. SDA was being treated like just another asset class. We knew it needed a different approach.

Although SDA has added complexity compared to residential development, the basics still apply. Good design matters. So does build quality, location, and functionality. What makes SDA different is the outcome. You're creating homes for people with real needs. If you make a poor design choice, it can have a direct impact on someone's quality of life. As developers, we also need to look at the big picture in regards to commercial impact. Elements including risk, finance, investor return, etc., are also relevant considerations that need to be balanced amongst all those things.

That's what guides us now. We don't build with a 'mere' compliance mindset; it's about compliance but so much more. We focus on building homes that are thoughtful, functional, and genuinely suited to the people who will live in them. That takes more time. It takes greater understanding. It takes better conversations. But it's worth doing properly.

What Makes a Developer in the SDA Space

There's often confusion about what a property developer actually does. Some people think it's about building houses. Others assume it's about finance. In reality, a developer is the person who holds the full vision of a project. Our job is to bring together all the moving parts and make sure they lead to one clear outcome.

Property development, at its core, is about adding value. That could mean building from scratch, changing the use of a site, getting a planning approval, or upgrading an existing property. The developer is the one responsible for organising all the elements that make that value possible. We deal with the site, the money, the design, the approvals, the consultants, and the construction. We don't need to be experts in every area, but we do need to know how to bring experts together and keep them aligned and working effectively.

That's where the real challenge comes in. Every specialist involved in a project brings their own priorities. Finance is focused on feasibility. Builders are thinking about materials and timeframes. Town planners are looking at zoning and compliance. If those perspectives aren't managed well, they can clash. And if you let one group dominate the conversation, you can end up with a project that doesn't work for all stakeholders.

My role as the developer is to make sure the final outcome is the outcome we should strive for (or we'll get to a place where we don't want to be) and that all the decisions along the way are in alignment with this vision. I need to understand enough about each area to make informed decisions, but not be pulled too far into one lens. That means knowing when to push back and when to take advice. It also means asking the right questions early and keeping everyone accountable to the same goal.

SDA adds another layer to this because you're not just thinking about financial return or aesthetic appeal; you're also designing for functionality, safety, and the comfort of people who often have very specific needs. That doesn't mean you throw everything else out; it means you have to make different trade-offs that are suitable for 'this' project.

When it works, it's because every person involved understands the outcome we're aiming for. You need a builder who respects the detail, a town planner who understands flexibility, and a designer who knows designs for the end user – the SDA participants and supported independent living (SIL) providers who use the dwelling. My job is to connect those dots and make sure nothing gets lost along the way.

That's what being a developer really means. You hold the whole picture, from the dirt to the front door.

It's Just Different Housing

There's a tendency in this space to treat SDA like it's something separate from the rest of the property world. People act like you have to forget everything you know about residential development and start from scratch. I don't agree with that. SDA isn't a mystery; it's still housing. It just needs to be done properly with the added nuance of SDA built on top of sound property development fundamentals.

I see SDA as a product type. Just like a childcare centre or a student accommodation building, it has its own requirements. That doesn't mean you throw out the fundamentals of good design. People are still going to live there. They still need comfort, privacy, light, ventilation, and flow. Those needs don't change just because it's a specialist property.

In fact, the best SDA homes I've seen are the ones that don't look or feel like a facility. They feel like real homes. You walk in and immediately get a sense that someone could build a life there. It's not about being clinical or high-tech for the sake of it; it's about creating a place that works for people with different abilities without losing the warmth and practicality that every home should have.

One of the mistakes I see often is developers becoming too caught up in the SDA design guidelines. Don't get me wrong, they're essential. But they're one of the many things that matter. Just because something meets the guideline doesn't mean it's good. You still need to think about how the home is going to function day to day. Is there enough natural light? Where will people store their belongings? Is the home easy to move through, not just on paper, but in real life?

Another issue is that people forget how quickly this market is evolving. For a while, anything that was built in

SDA was filled. That won't last. In the 2025/26 market we are already seeing the shift. As more stock hits the market, participants will have choice. Providers will compare options. That means quality and overall function will start to matter more than ever.

If you build something cheap or something that feels institutional, it might technically qualify as SDA, but when better homes are available, no one will choose yours. There's always a demand for quality. The goal should be to build something you'd be proud to live in yourself.

SDA isn't special; it's just good property development done with more thought and more responsibility.

Designing for a Real Person

People often ask whether we design SDA homes for a specific participant or just follow the general categories in the guidelines. The answer sits somewhere in between. You can't design for one person because that creates too much risk if they leave, but designing for nobody in particular doesn't work either. We approach it by creating an avatar—a type of person who might live there—then building around their likely needs.

You have to understand what the home is meant to do. That includes the participant, but also the SIL provider, the support workers, and anyone else who interacts with the space. Each group brings a different set of needs, and sometimes those needs conflict. Part of the job is deciding which trade-offs make sense for the long-term use of the home.

You also need to look at what else is being built. If a suburb already has a flood of HPS apartments, building more of the same won't help anyone. You end up with oversupply in one category and unmet demand in another. That's where developers can either add value or add noise. Too often, it's the latter.

It's the same thinking you'd apply in any other product development process. What do people want? What's already available? Where is there a gap? Sometimes the best designs come from solving problems people haven't been able to articulate yet. You build something and they say, 'This is just what we've been looking for.' That's what you aim for.

There are also technical limits. Planning controls, building codes, and the SDA Design Standard will shape what you can and can't do. Some ideas won't get past council. Others don't work on certain blocks. You're constantly making adjustments to get the best result within the real-world constraints.

The goal is to build something that makes sense now but also holds value in the future. If someone moves out, another participant should be able to move in without major changes. That's what makes the development sustainable.

You're designing for people, but not just one person. If you get it right, you create something that continues to serve well beyond the first tenancy.

Compliance is Just One Layer

A lot of people come into SDA thinking it's all about the design guidelines. They focus on the checklist and forget that the checklist is just one part of the equation. Compliance is important, but it's not the full picture. Meeting the standard doesn't mean you've created a good home; it just means you've cleared the minimum bar.

SDA is residential development with extra layers. You still have to work within the local planning rules, building codes, and environmental overlays, just like any other project. Then you have the SDA-specific requirements on top. The challenge comes when those layers don't align. That's where the complexity starts to show up.

For example, the SDA design guideline might call for a particular room size or layout, but the local council might restrict your building footprint in a way that makes that impossible. Or the access requirements in the SDA specifications might conflict with the setbacks required by planning. You're constantly balancing one rule against another and working out where you can make it fit.

The key is to treat compliance as a base layer. It gives you the framework, but not the answers. You still need to think about how the home will actually be used. Will it be comfortable? Will it make sense for support workers delivering care? Is it designed in a way that respects privacy and dignity? None of that is addressed directly in the guidelines, but it's just as important.

We've had projects where we had to apply for variations or negotiate with councils for months just to get one element approved. A 200-millimetre change in a setback might not seem like much, but in a bedroom that needs to meet SDA dimensions, it can be the difference between passing and failing. That kind of pressure is constant in this space.

You also have to remember that town planners aren't thinking about participant outcomes. Their job is to apply the planning rules. If you come to them talking about care needs or quality of life, it won't help your application. You need to speak their language. Show them how you still meet the intent of the policy, even if you're not following it word for word.

SDA has its own constraints, but that's just part of development. The real work is in knowing how to navigate those layers without losing sight of why you're building the property in the first place.

The Art of Translating Feedback

One of the most misunderstood parts of SDA development is how feedback is gathered and used. Everyone says you need to talk to SIL providers, and that's true, but not all feedback is helpful. In fact, most of it isn't.

I've spoken to at least 20 SIL providers to get input on design. Out of those, maybe 15 pieces of feedback were completely useless. It's not that people are being difficult; it's that most don't know how to read a plan, and they're often reacting to things they don't fully understand. You show someone a drawing, and they picture something completely different from what's going to be built.

That's not their fault. Visualising space from a two-dimensional plan is a skill. Most people can't do it, and even people in the industry get it wrong. So when a provider says they want a bigger bedroom or a different bathroom layout, the first question I ask is 'Why? What problem are they trying to solve?'

Sometimes there's a real insight behind the comment. Maybe they've supported someone who uses a shower bed, and the standard HPS bathroom is too tight for that. That kind of feedback is valuable. But most of the time, people are just repeating what they're used to or throwing in preferences without context.

The important thing is knowing how to translate what people say into something meaningful for the project. You can't take every comment at face value. You need to sit down, ask questions, and understand the lived experience behind the suggestion. That's when you start hearing things that actually matter.

This process can't be done over email. Real-world experience and understanding are crucial to the process. You need real conversations. You need to visit existing homes, watch how support is delivered, and see where things flow well and where they break down. That's where the real design insights come from. The things people do without thinking often reveal more than what they say.

It's also worth remembering that the end user is not just the SIL provider; it's the participant. Sometimes those needs conflict. What's efficient for care staff might not feel right for the person living there. You have to make judgment calls and decide which trade-offs are acceptable.

I don't assume I know everything. I've never lived with a disability. I haven't supported someone with their daily routines. I rely on people who have, but I filter everything through the goal of creating a home that works for everyone involved.

Feedback is essential, but it's not all equal. The skill is in knowing what to take on and what to leave behind.

Watching How People Use Space

If you want to know whether a home works, don't ask someone, watch them use it. That's where the real answers are. You can talk through plans, swap emails, run workshops, but nothing beats walking through a space and seeing how people interact with it.

We've done a lot of that. I've walked SDA homes with carers, participants, and support coordinators. What they notice in real time is completely different from what you get when you ask them to review a floor plan. A carer might point out how tight the bathroom really is when helping someone shower. A participant might show you how hard it is to open a cupboard from a seated position. These things don't come up on paper.

Even within a project team, different people see different things. I'll walk through a build with a construction hat on and notice things about layout and finish. Then I'll walk through the same space with someone in care, and they'll pick up issues I hadn't even thought about. That kind of cross-feedback is gold. It's the difference between guessing and actually learning.

We've also seen it play out over time. When someone has lived in a house for a few months, they'll tell you what works and what doesn't. You see what is used, what is ignored, and what needs adjusting. That kind of feedback is more valuable than any guideline. It's based on reality, not theory.

Most people don't know exactly what they want until they've lived in a space. We've seen that even with custom residential builds. Clients will spend months planning their dream layout and still say later, 'I wish I'd done this differently.' That's just how it is. Living in a space reveals what matters. This is why show homes and walkthroughs are so useful. It's one thing to look at drawings; it's another to physically move through a hallway or try to reach a light switch. If you're designing SDA without ever watching how it's used, you're missing half the story.

We take all that on board as we move from one project to the next. Design is never finished. It's a process of learning, testing, and refining. Observation tells you more than any checklist. That's how you get better at building homes that actually work.

Assistive Tech isn't Fancy

There's a lot of noise about technology in SDA, but it's not about being high-tech or cutting-edge. The role of assistive tech is to make life easier. That's it. It should support the way someone lives, not get in the way.

As developers, our job isn't to choose the devices. We focus on the structure that allows for different setups. That means thinking ahead. We install proper cabling, power points, and systems that can support whatever the participant needs now or in the future. Once the house is finished, we're not involved anymore, so everything has to be ready from the start so that the resident can live comfortably from the beginning.

We work with automation consultants to help us design that infrastructure. It's not about guessing what technology someone will use; it's about making sure the home can support a range of possibilities. Some people will want voice control. Others might prefer push buttons, sensors, or eye-tracking tools. Our role is to make sure all of those are possible today and into the future, without needing to knock out walls later.

Some of the features we've seen include door openers, voice-activated lights, or kitchen benches that adjust up and down. None of this is new, but it works well when it's set up properly. The key is getting the base right: cabling, power supply, and layout. If those things are missing, everything else becomes harder or more expensive.

It's also important not to over-engineer. Not every feature needs to be installed upfront. What matters is that it can be added easily when needed. That's better for the participant, and it gives the SIL provider flexibility too.

We look at tech as part of basic function. A home that's ready for automation gives people more control over their environment. That can reduce the need for support and make things easier for everyone involved.

People often try to make tech more complicated than it is. Good SDA design doesn't need to be flashy; it just needs to be thoughtful. Get the structure right and the rest can be adapted later, based on who moves in and how they live.

Where Form Meets Function

In residential design, everyone talks about function and form. In SDA, that balance becomes even more important. The problem is, people often focus too much on one and forget the other.

Function isn't just about meeting turning circles or door widths. It's about how someone lives in the home. One of the biggest things I see missed is storage. Every SDA I've seen is undercooked in storage. Everyone's thinking about the bathroom layout, but no one's asking where the linen goes or where you're putting the vacuum cleaner. We need to look at it from an everyday usage point of view. That's real life. If it's not thought through, the home becomes hard to live in, even if it's compliant.

You also have to think about the finer details. Where are people putting their shoes when they come in? Is there enough room to move in the bedroom if a support worker is there? Are the doors swinging the right way? These seem like small things, but they affect the day-to-day use of the home, and without this foresight, the home can be unfit for its purpose.

At the same time, people want to live somewhere that looks good. No one wants to feel like they're living in an institution. The good thing is that the product range has improved. You can now find fixtures and fittings that are accessible and still look great. The challenge isn't availability; it's knowing how to put it together.

We work with interior designers who understand this. A good design team can make sure the home looks and feels like something you'd want to live in, not just because it's functional, but because it's comfortable, well-lit, and feels like a proper home.

This isn't about going over the top; it's about thinking through how the space is going to be used and making sure that everything has a place and a reason. You want someone to walk in and feel like it makes sense, not just technically, but emotionally too.

You can meet all the SDA guidelines and still build a bad house. Just because it passes doesn't mean it works. What I care about is whether someone moves in and wants to stay, whether or not it feels like a home. That's the test.

Lessons from the Field

Some of our early SDA projects are only reaching completion now. They're the first ones coming off the ranks in Perth, so we're starting to see how everything holds up. We've done a lot right, and we've also learned where the friction points are.

One of the best decisions we made was getting support early and keeping consultants engaged all the way through. We spent a lot of money on it, and this is something I'd do again. People think you just need to get an SDA assessor in at the end, sign off the checklist, and you're done. That's a gamble. What if the walls are wrong? What if something doesn't meet specifications and you can't fix it without ripping it out?

We had our certifiers come in at multiple stages: early slab checks, framing checks, and pre-handover walkthroughs. We weren't guessing. There were even times when something had been approved on paper, then flagged later once the assessor saw it built. That happens. Everyone's still working it out. You have to go in assuming something will be missed. That kind of productive paranoia is useful.

We also took the same approach with SIL and SDA providers. We engaged them early to get feedback on the designs. But most of the value comes from sitting down and talking through why they're asking for something. You're not there to take orders; you're there to figure out what needs to happen for the home to work.

Design is one part. Planning is another. That was probably the biggest headache. With SDA, you're always pushing the boundaries, literally. A bedroom needs a specific internal width to pass, and to get that, you might need to push the wall closer to the boundary. Now you've got a setback problem. We've had planning approvals take over a year because of that kind of back and forth.

You can't walk into those conversations and talk about quality of life or housing for people with disabilities. That doesn't mean anything in a planning context. The town planner wants to know if your design complies with the policy or if you've justified the variation clearly. That's it. You have to understand the boundaries of everyone's role and talk to them in their terms. Otherwise, nothing moves.

SDA projects have more variables. More moving parts. More opportunities for contradiction between different frameworks. You have to be across all of it and know where the pressure points are going to be. And still, something will go sideways. That's why you need to stay close to the project. Don't assume anything is sorted until you've walked it, measured it, and checked it.

We've got more confidence now, but we're still learning. Every build shows us something we didn't expect. You can either be rigid and frustrated, or you can pay attention and keep getting better. That's the only way to keep delivering better homes.

CONCLUSION: TURNING IDEAS INTO ACTION

BY TANIA GOMEZ

When I first started learning about SDA, I didn't know where to begin. I felt overwhelmed, and I've worked in the NDIS for over a decade as a teacher, provider, consultant, and auditor. If I was struggling, I knew others would be too.

That's why I started the SDA Mastery podcast—to ask the questions I couldn't find answers to and talk to people who were doing the work. This book came out of those conversations and the ongoing frustration of providers with the lack of information and education available in the sector.

It's not a polished framework or a how-to guide; it's a collection of insights from people figuring it out in real time. It's for providers who are trying to do SDA the best they can in a system that's far from perfect, and who need something real to help them along the way.

We've covered a lot in this book, and I want to take a moment to reflect on what you've just read.

What We Explored in This Book

In **Part 1: Beyond the Build**, we looked at what good SDA should be.

Joseph explained why following the rules doesn't guarantee you're delivering something meaningful. Dinesh brought it home with a powerful reminder that design impacts everyday freedom and independence. Keira showed us how flawed planning processes stop great projects before they even get off the ground.

In **Part 2: From Plans to Practice**, we moved into the day-to-day reality of being an SDA provider.

Bruce talked about dignity and how good design isn't always about more, but about making better decisions. I broke down the SDA Practice Standards in a way that makes sense on the ground. Perry shared the emotional and practical toll of stepping into SDA with good intentions and little guidance.

In **Part 3: The Road Ahead**, we zoomed out to the bigger system.

Hong unpacked how the data we use is shaping the wrong decisions. Brad explained how ethical investment is possible if we get the model right. Debbie reminded us that SDA is part of a bigger ecosystem and needs to be delivered alongside support. Angad wrapped it all up with practical advice on how to scale SDA without compromising quality.

All these chapters come back to one key theme—there's no single answer, but there's a better way. A way that puts people first, that learns from mistakes, and that's willing to speak up about what isn't working.

This book isn't the end of anything. It's something you can come back to when you need perspective, a new idea, or a bit of clarity. And it's just one part of what we've built to support you.

If this book made you feel less alone, if it gave you some direction, or even just made you feel seen, that means something. If you're still left with questions, that's okay. There are more places to go from here.

Your Next Step: Chapter-by-Chapter Actions

Choose one idea from each chapter and start applying it. Small shifts lead to big progress. Here's something practical you can do after every chapter:

Part 1: Beyond the Build

Chapter 1–Joseph Connellan
Next step: Review one of your current or planned SDA properties. Ask yourself if this house enables real choice and control, or is it just compliant? Talk to a tenant or participant and ask what 'home' means to them.

Chapter 2–Dr Dinesh Palipana
Next step: Map out how your housing supports independence and connection. Identify one thing you could improve: layout, lighting, access, or onboarding. Even small changes matter.

Chapter 3–Keira Nicholson
Next step: Before your next build, meet with your council or planning department. Identify the risks early. Write down three ways to make your next application smoother.

Part 2: From Plans to Practice

Chapter 4–Bruce Bromley
Next step: Walk through one of your SDA homes and ask yourself, 'Would I want a family member living here?' Bring someone with lived experience, if possible. Write down one change you'll make.

Chapter 5—Tania Gomez
Next step: Print out the SDA Practice Standards. Highlight where you feel strong and circle where you feel unsure. Use this to create a compliance action plan for the next 90 days.

Chapter 6—Perry Klepe
Next step: Reach out to someone newer in SDA and share one lesson you learned the hard way. If you're new yourself, list five questions you still have and book a call with someone who's done it before.

Part 3: The Road Ahead

Chapter 7—Hong Knowling
Next step: Review SDA demand data in your region. Are you building for what's needed or what feels easy? Identify one underserved location or participant group and research their needs.

Chapter 8—Brad Fuller
Next step: Write a one-page investor summary of your SDA model. Can you clearly explain your purpose, financial model, and impact? Ask someone to review it and give honest feedback.

Chapter 9—Debbie Kindness
Next step: Book a coffee with a support coordinator, therapist, or local service provider. Ask how you can work better together to support participants in housing?

Chapter 10—Angad Singh
Next step: Create your own internal quality checklist. Go beyond compliance. What are your standards for design, delivery, onboarding, and tenant experience? Share it with your team.

KEEP GOING WITH US

This book was written to support you, but it's not the only place you can learn.

Join our Provider Collective–our free online community where NDIS providers, including SDA and SIL providers, share ideas, get support, and learn together. Completely free to join at www.providercollective.com.au

Listen to the SDA Mastery Podcast–Hear from real providers, sector leaders, and lived experience voices–the messy, honest, helpful stuff.

Come to our events–From national summits to local masterclasses, everything we run is focused on helping you take action. Find these on Eventbrite or at taniagomez.com. au

Need guidance? Book a consult–If you want help with SDA compliance, documentation, audit prep, or just need to talk something through, book a free 15-minute call with me. Sometimes that's all it takes to get unstuck.

REACH OUT TO THE AUTHORS

This book brought together some of the most generous, honest people working in SDA today. They've been open about their wins and their lessons. If one of their chapters resonated with you, send them a message. Ask questions. Share what you're trying to build. They'll appreciate it. This sector needs more of that: more collaboration, more transparency, more lifting each other up.

> 'Alone we can do so little. Together
> we can do so much.'
>
> —Helen Keller

This book is a reminder that we're stronger when we show up together. That's how we make real change, not just for our businesses, but for the people we support and the homes we're building for them.

Let's keep going. Together.

Tania Gomez

FUTURE-PROOFING YOUR NDIS BUSINESS

Lessons in Leadership, Business Systems, and Innovation from Australia's Top Voices in the Disability Sector

WITH TANIA GOMEZ AND INDUSTRY LEADERS

FUTURE-PROOFING YOUR SIL (SUPPORTED INDEPENDENT LIVING) BUSINESS

Building Participant-First Homes, Strong Practices, and Independent Futures

WITH TANIA GOMEZ AND INDUSTRY LEADERS

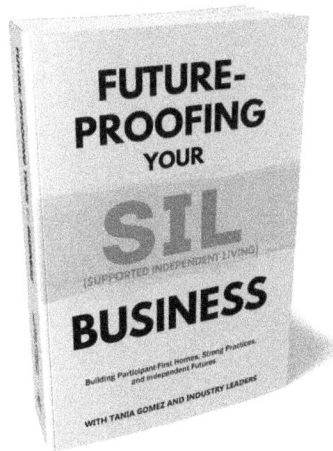

OTHER BOOKS BY TANIA GOMEZ
& INDUSTRY LEADERS